T0117660

"Move over, ayahuasca. Looks like the magic toad ride is the next big thing for entheogenic explorers."

—Don Lattin, bestselling author of *The Harvard Psychedelic Club*

"The author has had an astounding and intense life that he shares in his gentle and honest story. Most serious psychedelic explorers remain fixated on the psychedelic that first opened them to larger consciousness. Few people have had as much, as varied, and as meaningful psychedelic experiences. Given the sheer volume of his experiences, as he himself says, most people would've become insane. Instead, he became a practicing physician and now divides his time between his medical practice and helping people make the best possible use of the short acting, 'most powerful entheogen,' 5-MeO-DMT. His teaching is a gift, as is this book about it."

—James Fadiman, PhD, microdose researcher and author of *The Psychedelic Explorer's Guide: Safe, Therapeutic, and Sacred Journeys*

"Dr. Gerry is the Indiana Jones of the psychedelic world, as we join him in an adventure ever deeper down the rabbit hole to discover the long forgotten Holy Grail of psychedelics: 5-MeO-DMT, the God molecule."

—Alexander George Ward, shamanic artist, illustrator of *Ayahuasca Jungle Visions*

"Dr. Gerardo Sandoval's detailed account of his entheo-gen usage in *The God Molecule* takes the reader on a fascinating journey as he shares his personal experiences of self-discovery and transformation. His authentic approach to enlightenment is refreshing!"

    —Shelly Wilson, intuitive medium, conscious creator, and author of *28 Days to a New YOU, Connect to the YOU Within* and *Journey into Consciousness*

"Is there a 'God molecule,' and, if so, what are the effects of a deficiency of this precious substance? In its absence, our ambitious-but-destructive quest for meaning has led to the near undoing of the world. It's time to return to center, to glimpse the secrets that have resided within us all along. Let the bufo toad lead you home, and let Dr. Gerardo Ruben Sandoval Isaac lead you to the toad."

    —Daniel Vitalis, ReWild Yourself Podcast; founder of SurThrival.com

"Let the post-secular revelation revolution begin! Access to God is inside our brains through neurochemical pathways. Read Dr. Gerry's journey to truth and the infinite one in everyone."

    —Alex Grey, visionary artist

THE
GOD
MOLECULE

My Journey to 5-MeO-DMT
and the Spiritual Path to Divine Light

Gerardo Ruben Sandoval Isaac, MD, OB-GYN

DIVINE
ARTS

Published by DIVINE ARTS
DivineArtsMedia.com

An imprint of Michael Wiese Productions
12400 Ventura Blvd. #1111
Studio City, CA 91604
(818) 379-8799, (818) 986-3408 (FAX)

Editors: Geraldine Overton and Gary Sunshine
Layout artist: William Morosi
Cover Design: John Brenner
Cover Art: Justin Totemical © 2015, Totemical@gmail.com, http://www.totemical.com/
Printed by McNaughton & Gunn, Inc., Saline, Michigan

Note to the Reader: The information provided in this book is for educational, historical, and cultural interest only and should not be construed as advocacy for the use or ingestion of 5-MeO-DMT or other psychedelics. Neither the author nor the publisher assumes any responsibility for physical, psychological, or social consequences resulting from the ingestion of these substances or their derivatives.

Text set in 11-point Utopia with headings in 18-point Geogrotesque Semibold

Manufactured in the United States of America
Copyright 2016 by Gerardo Ruben Sandoval Isaac, MD, OB-GYN
All rights reserved. No part of this book may be reproduced in any form or by any means without permission in writing from the author, except for the inclusion of brief quotations in a review.

Library of Congress Cataloging-in-Publication Data

Names: Isaac, Gerardo Ruben Sandoval, 1979- author.
Title: The God molecule: 5-MeO-DMT and the spiritual path to divine
 light / Dr. Gerardo Ruben Sandoval Isaac; edited by Charles W. Mitchell.
Description: Studio City, CA : Divine Arts, 2016. | Includes bibliographical
 references.
Identifiers: LCCN 2015049481 | ISBN 9781611250497
Subjects: LCSH: Hallucinogenic drugs and religious experience. |
 Dimethyltryptamine.
Classification: LCC BL65.D7 I83 2016 | DDC 204/.2--dc23
LC record available at https://lccn.loc.gov/2015049481

*To the Cosmic Universal Light of Everlasting Love
(The Source) that lies within each and every one of us*

*To my best accomplishments in my life: my children; my three
brightest and most beautiful stars, Meztli Montserrat, Gerardo Miguel,
and Melissa Estefania. In hope that they find and see the Light of
Eternal Love and that somewhere someday we will be together*

*To my dear families, my brothers, my sisters, and all people
who became part of my life's project and all participants
of the ceremonies performed with this Light*

*To my parents, Ruben and Yolanda, my
grandparents Sara and Salvador*

*To my "little one" Sister Carla Sofia, and to
my dear cousin Veronika Rosas*

*To dear Jefa Margarita (RIP), Dona Carmen Contreras, and Aldo
Spera (RIP) and all the people of Los Catorce, San Luis Potosi*

*To the Family Cruz Pinacho and all the beautiful
people from San José Pacifico, Oaxaca*

To Mila Jansen from Amsterdam

To Don Alejandro Martinez from Bacalar

To Chicho Novelo and Edmund from August Pine Ridge, Belize

*To my dear friends Eduardo Diaz "wallo," Mario Cuevas
(RIP), Jovanni Vargas, Sensei Castaneda-san (RIP), Marco
Antonio Gonzalez, Gabriela Gomez Junco, Nicola Robinson,
Lisa Collins, Nora Gedgaudas, Mike Free, Christian Zuger
Andersen, Eva Brinch from Mon Island, Lomasa, Luis Ogarrio,
Odily Fuentes, Cayetano Luciano and Octavio Rettig*

*To all my teachers and pioneers of the Entheogenic Experience:
Aldous Huxley, William Burroughs, Albert Hofmann,
Richard Evans Schultes, Jonathan Ott, Alexander "Sasha"
Shulgin, Ralph Metzner, Terence and Dennis McKenna, Abe
Maslow, Alan Watts, Carl G. Jung, Bob Nasta Marley*

CONTENTS

Foreword   *x*

... Let There Be Light!   *1*

5-MeO-DMT: A Brief Chronology   *6*

The Search for the God Molecule   *8*

The Beginning   *10*

The Dream   *14*

Real de Catorce   *21*

The Peyote Experience   *34*

San José Pacifico   *49*

The Entheogenic Experience   *53*

The Lost Treasure   *67*

Medical School   *78*

Nepal and India   *86*

The Salvia Experiment   *93*

The Fall into the Pit   *99*

Bufo alvarius: The Sonoran Desert Toad   *107*

The Transfiguration   *116*

The Outcome   *120*

My Statement   *135*

Toad Message to the World   *140*

Bibliography   *143*

Vaporizing 5-MeO-DMT from
Bufo alvarius as an Entheogen:
A Retrospective Case Control Study   *148*

Seri Chants from the Comca'ac Nation,
Punta Chueca, Sonora, Mexico   *156*

Dr. Gerry's Invocation   *158*

About the Author   *160*

FOREWORD

5-MeO-DMT — the world's most powerful entheogen.

The crown jewel.

The God molecule.

The tool that allows us to experience the fullness of that which we truly are — the divine light of God that is the source and substance of all of reality.

The revelation of That Which Truly Is.

This is the story of one man's journey into the pure light of being. Like many who have experienced the grace and power of 5-MeO-DMT, in the form of the entheogenic secretions of the Sonoran Desert toad, Dr. Gerardo Ruben Sandoval Isaac has chosen to share this most profound experience with others, both through providing 5-MeO sessions with patients, and now, through this book.

He begins his story with his choice to seek after the magical peyote cactus, initiating his journey into the world of entheogens at the young age of thirteen. A seeker of knowledge, the as-yet-to-be Dr. Gerry dives fully into the quest for experience of the mystical, magical, and inner-knowing afforded by entheogens, pursuing LSD, psilocybin mushroom, and *Salvia divinorum,* while simultaneously earning a degree in medicine, ever seeking his place, his purpose, and the fullness of his being.

When events turn dark in his life, he eventually turns to more destructive substances, becoming addicted to crack. What turns his life around is his experience with 5-MeO-DMT, the most astounding entheogenic substance available to humanity. Now, he has embraced as his mission the sharing of the wonders of 5-MeO-DMT with the world. As he expresses it, now is the time that humanity needs this potent medicine more than ever.

If anything has the ability to help humanity turn the corner of its current misguided and destructive ways, it is 5-MeO-DMT. Nothing else has the power to so radically and effectively rip away the multilayered masks of illusion and false identity that humans have created for themselves, to starkly, lovingly, fiercely, and powerfully reveal the true divine nature of all reality. Underneath all the confusion, all the games, all the projections, the hate, the fear, the attachments, the judgments of self and other, there is only God — one eternal being of pure energy, light, awareness, and infinite love. It is the birthright of every human to experience this reality for him- or herself, for this is what we truly are, and 5-MeO-DMT is the ultimate tool for helping individuals realize this for themselves. This is a truth that cannot be taught, cannot be simply "believed" — it is something that can only be genuinely appreciated through the vehicle of direct experience. 5-MeO-DMT makes this possible in a way that is incomparable to any other method in its efficiency and immediacy.

Entheogens have the power to turn a life around. 5-MeO-DMT just might have the power to turn the world around. As Dr. Gerry writes, there is nothing that is "unnatural" in the unified reality that is God. 5-MeO-DMT radically affects human self-awareness and reveals something profound about reality. The key to understanding the origins of everything, including the individual self, is right here, and every human who desires it should inherently have the right to experience it. Anyone who has had the opportunity to experience 5-MeO-DMT knows this is it. This is the reality of who and what we are. The big bang, the divine light of creation and all being is right here, right now, in this experience, and lived in this very existence that each of us finds ourselves living through.

In the world of entheogenic literature, there are only a handful of authors who have written at any length on 5-MeO-DMT, such as myself, James Oroc, and Ralph Metzner. It is a pleasure to see that we can now add Dr. Gerry to the slowly growing list of those who would share knowledge of this most profound molecule with the world. This work here is personal, tragic, ecstatic, reckless, and healing. The entheogenic path of self-knowledge is always an unusual one, with many strange twists and turns along the way. For those committed to Truth and Genuine Being, however, it is invaluable, and holds the greatest of gifts, as Dr. Gerry learned — the revelation of the divine nature of everything and the universal self that is God. That such a profound gift can come from the secretions of a desert toad is perhaps one of the great cosmic curiosities of existence — who would have guessed that a toad might hold the key to the ultimate transformation of human life? As I wrote in my novel *Beyond Azara*, "No one suspects the toad."

It is a pleasure to see Dr. Gerry sharing his light, his life, and his insights with all of us through the vehicle of this book. The time is right for the world to know about 5-MeO-DMT, and having the perspective of a doctor who has passed through the rigors of his own journey, and his insight through healing others with 5-MeO-DMT, is an important addition to information about 5-MeO-DMT. We are perhaps on the precipice of a radical change in human cultures in the modern world — a time when entheogenic medicines are accepted, supported, and given the legitimacy that they so rightly deserve. Entheogenic medicines can assist in the healing of mental, emotional, and physical disorders. And most importantly, can help individuals transcend the false realities they have created for themselves, and assist in the ultimate healing that comes from direct experience of the divine nature of being. The time is now, and there is no time to waste. This is the healing the world needs, and we can thank Dr. Gerry for doing his part as a vehicle for the infinite light that we truly are.

Let there be light.

The toad is happy.

MARTIN W. BALL, PhD
Author of *Being Infinite: An Entheogenic Odyssey into the Limitless Eternal — A Memoir from Ayahuasca to Zen*

... LET THERE BE LIGHT!

The irradiation of a great thought or a powerful imagination in Man, determines an attractive whirlpool that gives origin to planets to the intellectual sun, and satellites to the planets. A great Man, in the sky of thought, is the Light of a Universe.

ELIPHAS LEVI
The Great Secret: Or Occultism Unveiled

It has been suggested that the visions induced by DMT are the result of this biophotonic light emission from our DNA, which makes it possible for shamans to access a vast library of common planetary knowledge being shared between all living things in this Gaian web of biophoton emissions.

In relation to the DMT experiences... the light present in biophoton emission and superradiance is assumed to originate from within the zero point field (ZPF).

Ervin Laszlo
The Connectivity Hypothesis (2003)

Instead of an absolute space and time filled with ether that sustains the epiphenomenon of light, light becomes the fundamental thing whose propagation determines the flow of time and the weave of distance. We can almost say that light creates space-time. I suggest here that light, in the form of a universal electromagnetic zero point field, also creates and sustains the world of matter that fills space-time. Thus the words "Let there be Light" from the Bible may express more than a poetic mythology after all.

Bernard Haisch
The God Theory (2006)

We are in fact made up of light: every atom in our body (and our world) originated in the last gasp of a dying star, which threw the remains of its energy out into the galaxy in a cloud of rare elements....

We are beings of light, created and sustained by a star. Every culture has intuitively recognized this and credited that light is the source of our own divine nature....

Mystics since the beginning of time have attributed an understanding of the divine knowledge of that light, and the two have become inexorably entwined.

THOM HARTMANN
The Last Hours of Ancient Sunlight:
The Fate of the World and What We Can
Do Before It's Too Late (1999)

The information our brain receives originates not only in our body, but comes from all over the world. The brain's ten billion neurons, with 10,000 connections each, constitute the most complex system of electronic organization in the known universe. This system, which operates at the edge of chaos, receives and transforms information from our own body, as well as the electromagnetic acoustic and other wave fields in our environment. It also receives and decodes information from more subtle fields, including the vacuum's ZPF. Potentially, our brain connects us with the wide reaches of the cosmos.

ERVIN LASZLO (1997)

Since light travels at the speed of light, let's imagine a disembodied observer (pure mind with no mass) travelling at the speed of light. Einstein's equations would predict that, from light's own point of view, it travels no distance and takes zero time to do so. This points out towards something very strange indeed about light. Whatever light is, it seems to exist in a realm where there is no before and no after. There is only now.

PETER RUSSELL

From Science to God: A Physicist's Journey into the Mystery of Consciousness (2005)

[W]hen mind is free of its interface with matter, it has the capacity to move faster than the physical speed of light. Then time and space (as we experience them) would no longer exist....

This is the ultimate light, the light of creation, of mysticism, of religion, of information. As my consciousness leaves the confines of the physical world... and resonates in reunion with its original source, I briefly cease to exist except as that light. In the classical mystical sense — the light and I are one.

JAMES OROC, *Tryptamine Palace* (2009)

5 methoxy N,N- dimethyltryptamine is a member of the tryptamine family — a group of compounds that all have a basic tryptamine indole ring structure and are chemically related to the amino acid tryptophan.

The tryptamines are a fascinating branch of chemistry for human research since they include many biologically active compounds including both neurotransmitters and entheogens.

ALEXANDER SHULGIN
Tihkal (1997)

5-MeO-DMT:
A BRIEF CHRONOLOGY

>2000 years BCE	Evidence of humans using DMT in Central and South American snuffs
1855	First report of ayahuasca use
1931	DMT first synthesized by Richard Manske
1936	5-MeO-DMT is synthesized
1956	Stephen Szara reports psychedelic effects of DMT
1963	5-MeO-DMT isolated from *Anadenathera peregrina* or yopo seeds from Amazon Indian snuffs
1965	5-MeO-DMT discovered in the venom of the *Bufo alvarius* toad

1960s	Nick Sand discovers synthetic DMT could be smoked
1960 – 1970s	William Burroughs injects himself with DMT
1970	DMT, LSD, and mescaline classified as schedule I drugs in the Controlled Substances Act
1990s	Richard Strassman FDA approved clinical trials
2001	*The Spirit Molecule* published
2004	My first DMT experience
2005	My first 5-MeO-DMT experience
2006	My first toad hunt in the Sonoran Desert
The present	5-MeO-DMT is Schedule I in the US and restricted in Denmark, Germany, Greece, Japan, New Zealand, Sweden, Switzerland, and the UK.

THE SEARCH FOR THE GOD MOLECULE

I am a medicine man who had to face my own disease, my own demons, and experience multiple deaths, in order to fully heal myself by taking my own medicine. Only then could I begin to realize my larger dream: to harness the power of my personal discoveries and begin to help heal humanity.

The journey that led me to the God molecule, 5-MeO-DMT, is that of a human being on the hunt for divinity. Ever since I realized at a young age that we are born into a sick society that needs deep-root healing, my search for God, truth, love, and the true Light has defined my life. As you will learn from the pages that follow, this long and arduous trek began with my doubting the Catholic religion into which I was born. My education continued with the bitter lessons of the sacred peyote cactus, the aggressive teachings of the sacred landslide mushroom, all the way to the top of the pyramid when I first "kissed" the Sonoran Desert toad and reached the crown jewel: the God molecule, 5 Methoxy dimethyltryptamine.

It was through this journey that I was able to ask and answer the most fundamental questions: Who am I? What am I? Even though my life exposed me to many different paths, it was only through 5-MeO-DMT, the God molecule, that I was able to experience total ego dissolution and the full union of the Self with God/ infinity/eternity.

As humans we have always felt distant from the Whole, forced to believe that we were expelled from the Garden of Eden, obliged to build a concrete jungle in which we have to survive. Reality describes a world filled with fear, pain, and suffering. Entheogens — plants that give us visionary experiences — provide the means to feel we are part of something divine, something way bigger than what our human mind is capable of creating. A life filled with joy and meaning. The God molecule gives humans the chance to feel that we are connected to everything that is and that will always be. It is our ticket back home.

THE BEGINNING

I was born in the conservative city of Guadalajara, in the state of Jalisco, Mexico, on a cold night on the 15th of February 1979. I came early into this world, barely seven months into my mother's pregnancy, and already I wanted to see everything with my own eyes. My mother recalls the visit of Pope John Paul II to our city during this time. My mom lived very close to a monastery that the pope planned to visit. So she decided to go out in the street to watch him up close and personal. She recalls the pope seeing her and making a stop and touching her belly (me). He smiled at her and gave her his customary slight slap on the cheek as a token of appreciation. My mom said I immediately started to kick; she began to have slight contractions that got worse to the point that I gave my mom a premature delivery exacerbated by two large benign tumors on her uterus that constantly pressured me.

"Too premature," they said. I began my life, my first three months of life, in the pediatrics ICU. I was born too premature, with severe jaundice. I was kept under direct UV light with a small bandage covering my eyes, totally naked, to fight the liver insufficiency of my prematurity; my mom offered me her breast and I did not know what to do with it. I was too premature to have developed the instinct of sucking. So small that my mother told me I used to fit in a shoebox. "He is not going to make it," nurses commented to themselves. But mom kept faith and everyday brought me my breast milk and passed it through a catheter into my belly through my mouth, and talked endlessly as if I understood everything.

"Why do you talk to him?" a nurse asked her. "He is going to be very smart, I know it," she replied. If only she had known. As if she knew of my purpose. But any true mother has this maternal instinct of doing everything for her offspring.

Raised in high society and educated in the best schools money could buy, I learned English along with my mother tongue, Spanish, starting at age three, by private tutoring.

I did my fifth year of elementary school in the US, won the "*Optimus*" award for best student out of three hundred and sixty, and got a dozen medals for being the most outstanding student at Oaklawn Academy in Edgerton, Wisconsin, from 1989 to 1990.

I learned to speak, write, and read some Japanese (both native alphabets Hiragana and Katakana and very little kanji) at age twelve, Italian at fifteen, and a bit of German (while I lived in Bad Godesberg during my postgraduate studies) and a bit of Nahuatl (Aztec tongue).

So I am lucky in a way that I was born in a privileged social class, traveled around the world to more than twenty-five countries, and learned from different cultures; for a Mexican I was indeed lucky... I am Lucky Gerry.

Ever since I came to this world I was surprised by the amount of suffering and dissatisfaction in which humanity lived. Even though I got the best toys an ordinary Mexican boy could have, I wanted something different... something I did not get at home. Both my parents were workaholics and only came home to eat and sleep. So my sisters and I pretty much learned stuff on our own by comparing and questioning what we learned at school.

I felt and resented my parents' absence. I would have traded all my toys for quality time with them. But as people say, "one never chooses his parents." I was affected by poverty, sicknesses, pain, unfairness, and just like tiny Buddha, I had to do something about it... no matter what. I decided to "stop the World," as Carlos Castaneda mentioned in his book *The Teachings of Don Juan.*

THE DREAM

By age twelve, I started having repeated dreams. I am very fond of the Mexican pre-Hispanic cultures; I was amazed at their vision of the cosmos and their religious aspects. It was fascinating stuff for me. I loved going to the pyramids in my country. I knew there was a lost connection that needed to be found.

I started having a repeated dream. I dreamt of walking for hours in the desert in search of peyote. "Funny," I thought. I didn't even know what that was and yet I kept dreaming of it. So I went to my dad's library and looked over the *Encyclopedia of Mexico* and read about it.

> **Peyote.** (n) from the Aztec word "*peyotl*," refers to a hallucinogenic cactus that grows in Northern Mexico and the Southwestern US, used by the Indians in their rituals and ceremonies to communicate with their gods and deities. Also called *jucuri* or *hikuri* meaning "Light of God" by the Huichol and Raramuri Indians.

Lophophora williamsii, peyote cactus

"Unreal!" I thought. I immediately asked our maid about it and to my surprise she told me that she lived very close to a place where many "gringos" and foreigners go to eat peyote, Real de Catorce. Inspired by my impulsive personality, I immediately organized a short trip to this place, telling my parents that I would spend the weekend at my best friend's house.

So there I was in the Guadalajara Bus Station for the adventure of my life and only thirteen years old. My first adventure on my own! Suddenly a funny-looking guy, skinny with long hair, dressed in white cotton clothes, wearing a necklace made of flowers, stepped in front of me and asked if I was going to Real de Catorce. *How would he know?* I thought to myself. He was a Hare Krishna named Ricardo. As he introduced himself, he told me he had been going to the desert for some time now on a regular basis to eat peyote and he was willing to show me around and recommend a place to stay.

"Cool," I said. I could not have planned it better.

After a twelve-hour bus ride we finally made it to Estación Catorce in San Luis Potosi, a train station in the middle of the desert in front of the mountains of Sierra de Catorce. The train went from Laredo, Texas, to Mexico City and back.

It was 1994. He told me there were only two places to stay at Estación Catorce: "Jefa" Margarita's place or Dona Saba's. Both offered a room and a public bathroom for a dollar per day. Famous *peyoteros* or peyote seekers stayed in these places, making a pseudo community of psychedelic people who would share experiences in a common space.

We stayed at Jefa's place. Jefa ("chief") Margarita was an old woman blinded by smoky flames in a fire started, according to the locals, by *peyoteros* smoking reefer on the farm. In an attempt to save her farm animals, she lost her eyesight long ago.

She used to stay in the main entrance room, assisted by *peyoteros* who would negotiate the service for a place to sleep and food on a dish. Obviously, she was being robbed constantly.

I introduced myself to her and told her I was a first-timer and wanted to eat peyote. She told me that I needed to take the main road going to the desert valley and in just an hour or so of walking I would find myself surrounded by peyote.

I agreed to walk with the Hare Krishna. He taught me to sing the holy name chant so my mind would not lose itself to distractions in this special sacred place called "Wirikuta" by the Huichol Indians. The Huichol Indian tribe lives in the state of Jalisco, my home state. Every year they make a pilgrimage from the Jalisco Northern Mountains to the Wirikuta desert to collect the sacred peyote. Wirikuta means "sacred land."

So I chanted Hare Krishna's song while we entered Wirikuta, the Huichol name for the magical desert of Real de Catorce.

Ricardo told me as soon as I saw my first peyote (a beautiful feeling, by the way; none are the same, like blue stars lying on the desert floor) that I should ask permission to the peyote entity and never cut the first one. One must leave it as an offering, which I did and minutes afterward I saw literally hundreds if not thousands of peyote all around us, even stepped on some accidentally. I cut twelve peyotes and decided to eat eight of them... "Eat them in pairs," he advised.

The peyote cactus is the bitterest thing in the whole world! At first not so much but eventually the tongue starts to develop sensitivity toward the taste, until it becomes an almost impossible mission to swallow it.

Not to mention the nausea it evokes. Upon arriving at the stomach it immediately turns into bitter greenish foam that distends the stomach and makes it very easy to throw up. If one vomits it before absorption, it won't have an effect.

I learned that a minimum of an hour and a half of holding the peyote inside was sufficient to have a psychedelic experience regardless if one vomits afterward.

It is important not to drink many fluids because it will be easier to vomit.

I started to feel nausea and we decided to head back to the train station. Once we arrived at Estación Catorce the peyote started to kick in. All the colors in my vision became brighter, shining in a peculiar way. I started to see an aura on all things, and a huge sensation of well-being surrounded me.

I had lived that experience somewhere before. A huge déjà vu! It was just too familiar.

I could see and feel things before they happened. It was awesome.

The peyote showed me what was going to be the beginning of a long spiritual path. But for now that was

Three peyote buttons in Wirikuta. The smaller ones are "royal" *hikuris*, Carlos Castaneda's favorite, mentioned in *The Teachings of Don Juan*.

it, just a glimpse of a vision. Not much of the mystical experience I was longing for, even though it was magical waking up to life.

"I have to return to this place with more time," I thought. "Lots of study needs to be done here."

I ended up bouncing back to Real de Catorce every three months (that's how long the light of the experience would last for me).

I started reading Ouspenski, Gurdjieff, Aldous Huxley, C. Jung, A. Watts, A. Maslow — amazing texts!

I became an avid reader of Carlos Castaneda and all subjects related to hallucinogens (Timothy Leary, Gordon Wasson) and shamanism (Mircea Eliade). My most prized printed books at that age were *The Mystical Experience* and *The Doors of Perception*.

I was also amazed by the occult and became a huge fan of Eliphas Levi's masterpiece, *The Great Secret: Or Occultism Unveiled*.

All the kids in school thought I was a weirdo, a freak. I became a fan of The Doors and Pink Floyd music. Ambient New Age music, like The Orb, came on the scene with songs like "Fluffy Clouds" and colored my first mescaline trips.

So with puberty, my conservative parents' attempts to assert control over my life were just too much for my free soul. I exploded and ended up leaving home at age fifteen. I sold all my things and headed to the only place on Earth I wanted to be: Real de Catorce.

REAL DE CATORCE

Locals tell of a tale of fourteen ("Catorce") bandits who constantly robbed and attacked all stagecoaches or caravans that took the South-North trail through the state of San Luis Potosi. Apparently, they had their hideout deep in the mountains. When authorities finally decided to put an end to these

View of the city of Real de Catorce, SLP, Mexico

outlaws, they hunted them down to their hideout. Then they realized that at night, strange blue flames would appear, signaling the presence of precious metals underground. The place was immediately mined and became the most important mining site in the history of early Mexico; the first Mint House in Real de Catorce was built along with the first Mexican telephone connecting to the capital of Mexico City.

There was so much gold and silver in Real that slaves were brought in to do the mining and were obliged to live around the mine. The working class was limited to an area known as Los Catorce in the middle of the mountains where the mines were, and the "royal" class built a city at the top of the mountains later named Real de Los Alamos de La Purisima Concepcion de los Catorce, or simply "Real de Catorce."

The railroad arrived and replaced the stagecoaches by a safer trade route that connected Northern and Southern Mexico. Real de Catorce produced the largest silver and gold yields in the country in the late 1800s, and it was not until the Mexican Revolution started that chaos began to rule the place.

There is even a popular saying that goes: "*De aqui... pal Real*" which translates to "from here toward Real." It is used among people to say that from now on things will be different, hopefully better.

During the chaos of the revolution the working class "mined the mines," so to speak, by flooding them. No longer able to exploit the mines, the royal class bailed out and abandoned the city. The working class had nowhere to go and eventually populated the area.

There is archaeological evidence that suggests that men have been coming to Wirikuta for thousands of years! Their sanctuary or sacred mountain lies just minutes from the city of Real de Catorce. I found some cave paintings with drawings of peyote trips dating back thousands of years.

Real de Catorce is now quite a tourist attraction, a ghost town in the middle of the desert mountains in the heart of Mexico, marked by an abandoned mine. One can appreciate five kinds of people who come to the place. The locals, descendants of the working mining class; the Mexican *peyoteros*; the Huichol Indians; the foreign tourists; and a peculiar kind of Catholic tourist who comes to Real because its church is actually the sanctuary of St. Francis of Assisi.

Every October 3rd the followers of St. Francis celebrate his day with local festivities. Coincidentally, this date is the time that Huichol Indians arrive to Wirikuta to collect their peyote cacti and trek to their sacred mountain to carry out the ceremony of Thanks and Praise for a good peyote harvest and a good rainy season (a Huichol thanksgiving), making Real de Catorce a peculiar place indeed.

It was in this magical place that, as a sixteen-year-old, I decided to live with my dog, a Labrador named Jimbo, and a singular will to find myself, answer my questions, and discover the meaning of my dream/life and my first experience with the peyote.

I stayed at Jefa's place. She had a *zaguan* composed of eight rooms full of psychedelic drawings depicting the colorful trips of all people who stayed there. All rooms shared a central patio. The rent fee was ten pesos per night (slightly less than a dollar). I paid for a month in advance and was offered the central room, kindly called the Huichol room for a painting of a Huichol Indian eating peyote. My neighbor on my right side was a peculiar-looking guy claiming to be a shaman and artisan of Indian handcrafts, who went by the name of "Charly." On my left side was a junkie bird catcher who ate peyote to fight the addictive anxiety of smoking crack. Such characters in this comedy!

During my first week living in Estación Catorce I met a very interesting person from the Sonoran Desert, a Seri Indian descendant named Cayetano Luciano, who arrived at Jefa's place. Cayetano invited me to the desert for a peyote hunt. I agreed and while we entered the desert, he taught me a potent Seri power-song. He managed to make me memorize it completely and by the second hour we were both chanting the Seri words. "*Haya Haya otac ferenze marevaya ma, Haya Haya otac ferenze marevaya ma, Haya seya revaya ma, Haya Haya otac ferenze marevaya ma... Oka! Toyopotei!*" we sang. It went on and on. We raised the tone of the chant to a climax that enhanced our awareness. I was very excited and felt an unusual pep as I walked within the magical places of the Wirikuta desert. We found a good peyote spot, cut the peyote we needed, and headed back to Estación Catorce.

Once back at Jefa's place we ate the rest of our peyote and I saw in my vision that if I closed my eyes, a colorful snake continuously unrolled, came close to me, and showed me sacred geometry and incredible ancient desert knowledge.

Cayetano Luciano told me he had been sent by the local power-woman or shamaness who periodically performed ceremonies on Isla Tiburon in Sonora. He was sent to collect peyote for his Seri tribe. He showed me chants of the shamaness recorded on audiotapes. He was very proud of her, and of his tribe. Sadly, the next morning "someone" had stolen his audiotapes while we were making breakfast in the common kitchen, and feeling disoriented he decided to return to Sonora.

Later that night my bird-catcher crackhead-fiend neighbor started to play those audiotape cassettes in his room. I was very angry. I was to be very careful with him, though. He was evil. He eventually bailed out after having a dispute over some crack and pills and had to take the night train out of there. I was relieved. Now I only had "Charly" to talk to and the occasional *peyote-ros* to share our experiences.

I became a friend of Carlos, or "Charly," as he liked to be called, the pseudo-shaman who was more like a drug addict, fond of pre-Hispanic tribes, peyote, and pretty much anything that got you "high." He told me stories of the Huichol Indians, the shamans, and peyote trips.

I started to eat peyote on a regular basis, eating a full-dose trip every three days, at least every week-end, meeting people from all over the world. Ending up walking with many in the desert and showing them the peyote cactus, how to cut it, and how to eat it, I eventually became a young desert guide.

I had my own theories on how a plant such as peyote had evolved to its unique hallucinogenic features. I had thought that deserts were places full of minerals and "radioactive" materials. Maybe this radiation altered the DNA of a cactus, making it able to produce mescaline.

Or maybe it came from another planet by means of an asteroid, as Charly once mentioned. He said that many years ago a huge meteor struck the area known afterward as Wirikuta, and the tribes that witnessed the cosmological event went to the place it landed. To their surprise they saw a new "life-form" growing beside the meteor: the first peyote. Of course I laughed my guts out telling him he had smoked too much reefer. Ignorance is bliss.

After a while I got the hang of walking in the desert and recognized certain places worth going to. Even though to the naked eye everything looks the same, the desert varies so much; even the ground changes. I discovered places full of fossils, areas full of quartz, and regions with many aerolites, fragments of meteors. I also uncovered some hills full of *chuzos* or arrowheads from the ancient nomadic tribes that roamed Wirikuta long ago.

People accepted me in their society and, thanks to my Labrador, who enchanted all local kids, I was offered land for me to build my house.

I became an *ejidatario* (land-owner), built my home at age sixteen, became a legal adult at eighteen, and lived peacefully in Los Catorce.

I was offered El Galaviz, the place where, historically, the working class made their limestone for building. Besides a huge limestone oven there were two ruins, atop which I decided to build two adobe rooms with a small water deposit or pool.

I own a beautiful place in the middle of the mountains in Los Catorce, with the best view of the Wirikuta desert.

Curiously, on my birthday the sun sets exactly in the center of my view.

Of all the people coming to this magical place, either by train to Estación Catorce or by bus, eight out of ten were looking for a spiritual guide, a sort of "Don Juan" of Carlos Castaneda fame, to show them the way, take care of them, and guide them while having the peyote experience.

Eventually I became "famous" and no longer needed to go to the bus or train station to offer my guide services; instead, people from all over the globe arrived at Catorce and asked for "Gerry from Guadalajara."

If you had a good, satisfying experience, then it was assumed that you would spread the word and recommend me.

In less than two years as a tour guide I received people from Japan, New Zealand, Germany, the US, Israel, Italy, Argentina, Chile, Spain, Canada, and

My ranch in Los Catorce "El Galaviz," built at age sixteen

Switzerland — all of them asking for "Gerry" to guide them in the desert.

As a tour guide I ended up eating peyote with many people. I learned the hard way, having many bad trips and bad experiences with enough baboons, that one must not eat peyote with just anybody. I saw many cases of divine justice applied by peyote to people who did not have the respect for this plant, or for the experience it confers. These unfortunate individuals spent the entire trip trembling, cold, vomiting all the time, and asking for help to get "down" from it.

"The peyote teaches you the right way to live," the Huichol Indians say (an expression applied by the ethnobotanist Terence McKenna).

"Come peyote para que se quite lo pendejo," the Huichol also say, with a humorous tone ("Eat peyote so that you stop being an asshole" — more or less, although not a literal translation).

Each day I would wake up and go to the spring to fill my water supply, collect some firewood, start to warm some water for coffee, make breakfast, and begin a magical day at the mountains of Real de Catorce. Jimbo encouraged me to trek every single day. He loved

Gerry and Jimbo at the Huichol altar in Mt. Quemado, 1997

**Fresh sacred shrooms
from the Family *Psilocybe
caerulescens* var. *zapotecorum***

to trek, and if by any chance I would not decide to trek, he would take off without me and, happily moving his tail, would go down to Estación Catorce to hang out with the *peyoteros*. Sometimes he would return late at night very happy just to show off that he had a wonderful time at the desert at Jefa Margarita's place.

The tours that I provided included a visit to the sacred mountain of the Huichol Indians called Mt. Quemado, a trek to the Wirikuta desert for some peyote hunting, or a visit to the ghost town of Real de Catorce. We would even enter an abandoned mine to contemplate the stalactites or stalagmites. By the end of the day I would hang out with Panchito, a local from Los Catorce and my neighbor, and Aldo, sharing a tasty marijuana cigar and our daily chores and adventures. Aldo was an Italian who had been living for over twelve years in Real de Catorce. He was an artist who sculpted figures from rock and marble. He was like a father figure to me, even though he was always complaining about Mexicans, the weather... everything. For Aldo the world was a major fuckup, and all of us — excluding him — were responsible for it. I enjoyed watching him complain about everything. Talk about a frustrated old man.

I would light up a fire every single night, contemplating the skies, the stars, and just staring at the flames consuming the firewood. The Huichol Indians believe that an entity called Tatewari lives among fire. It was fascinating to watch the flames burn in an organized manner. If by any chance I had eaten peyote, it was really cool to watch silver lines that would connect every single star like a web, reminding me of Indra's Web from India. It was amazing to contemplate the interconnectedness that the peyote cactus shows you through its visions.

Even though one can obtain peyote or mescaline in the suburbs, or in Babylon, I would highly recommend having the experience in the desert, in its home or natural habitat. At night when the colors are more vivid and the light of the experience shines brighter, the sky is one of the many amazing things to gaze at while under the effect of peyote. One can literally see that all stars are connected.

Having the experience in the desert guarantees that it will be more entheogenic than visionary. By entheogenic, I mean that it will be an experience that recognizes God, recognizes God within, recognizes God in everything.

THE PEYOTE EXPERIENCE

T here are many published works regarding this wonderful medicine. I think Aldous Huxley's *The Doors of Perception* best describes the experience beyond words and since all experiences are personal, they have to be analyzed subjectively.

The peyote enhances our state of consciousness by increasing our awareness and affording us a more colorful view of our surroundings. It gives you a lot of pep. One can travel many miles without food or water by just eating peyote.

There are stories of Raramuri Indians catching deer on foot, or Tarahumara Indians climbing dangerous cliffs as mountain goats, that normally would be impossible for an ordinary human to accomplish.

After the difficult digestive process, and if one is lucky not to vomit, visions begin to appear according to our own light with a plateau lasting for up to twelve hours, featuring undulating psychedelic effects very similar to that experienced with LSD or mushrooms. I saw many Aztec symbols painted on every surface. I saw colorful patterns of jewel-like glowing that eventually turned into very vivid visions showing me what I needed to see.

I heard many testimonies of people seeing snakes, devils, and horrible visions demonstrating the negative nature of their own light. It is an actual projection of your own light filtered by your subconscious and your actions in life.

The ancients believed that the peyote shows you the right way to live by walking along your path like a brother without the punishing aggressiveness of the mushroom, and telling you, according to your history, whatever you need to do in your life to be a better person. It is very clear in its way of "telling things" using emotions rather than words. Using visions of our personal history is the way the peyote teaches us.

So good people will become better people, while negative people, well... they either enjoy what they see or complain about whatever this light is showing them, giving off a sensation that it "burns."

Even though geographically speaking the peyote spreads as far north as Oklahoma in the US, or as far south as the state of Queretaro or Puebla in Mexico, apparently it doesn't have the same effect in all places.

The peyote that grows just behind the Catorce Mountains in the valley of the city of Matehuala evokes drowsiness and puts you to sleep, rather than producing visions. The peyote in Queretaro just enhances awareness and gives pep but induces no psychedelic effects.

The Huichol Indians justify this with their meaning of Wirikuta or "Sacred Land," being this specific region chosen by their gods to create the world we know. Their Genesis narrative speaks of ancient gods gathering in Wirikuta to create the sun and summoning the spirit of Great Tamatz Kallaumari, the Elder Brother Blue Deer. Tamatz Kallaumari picked up the recently created sun with its horns and threw it to the skies, creating Night and Day. Afterward the blue deer disappeared in the desert, making peyote grow in every step it took.

It is with the spirit of Tamatz Kallaumari that we must follow its footprints manifested in peyote cacti through Wirikuta to reach God's light. So if one wanted to reach the light of true knowledge, one had to follow Tamatz Kallaumari into Wirikuta. A person who goes in is totally different after leaving Wirikuta, if he or she follows its teachings.

One of my first entheogenic experiences with peyote occurred during a visit with a person from my childhood days: my best friend, Eymos. We decided to drive into the desert rather than taking the long walk with Jimbo. I stopped at a place I thought was full of peyote. To our surprise there was none! We started to look for some on foot. Soon I realized I couldn't locate either Eymos or Jimbo.

I was lost! I couldn't even see the mountain ridge to locate the direction I was walking. Somehow I had managed to enter a small downhill valley where the mountains just disappeared. I got freaked out and started to run, coming to a sudden stop by one of the most painful thorns.

The desert is full of spines and thorny cacti. One must be very careful to know where to step. As I tried to pull out the spines, my skin would stretch to the point of unspeakable pain before releasing its thorn. Microscopically some desert thorns are actually hooks that hurt!

After catching a bunch of thorns, some of which I still carry under my skin today, I ended up sitting on a yucca palm looking at the sunset. I was crying, I had no jacket, no water, no matches, and I was completely lost. In an attempt to look up in the skies and scream for help, I noticed a bird flying over me. I thought it was an eagle and demanded that it show me the way out.

It was probably a vulture. It made a couple of circles and headed off. I followed it, and it eventually led me to the main road that brought me back to my dog and my friend.

I had just experienced a magical entheogenic experience without eating an entheogen. What a trip. I was amazed at Wirikuta's magic. This was no joke. And it was definitely not a hallucination. I had an encounter with God? The desert showed me that not everybody can find peyote. "Not everyone is invited to the Lord's supper," the Bible says.

Eymos told me that after getting lost he found my dog and it was by following him that eventually he found his way back to the road and to the car. Jimbo learned to travel eagerly in Wirikuta and became a very famous dog; from 1994 to 2000 everyone in Real de Catorce or Los Catorce or Estación Catorce knew who Jimbo was. Some of Jimbo's popularity was rooted in his leaving me for days. He would wake up in the morning and make his way down to Estación Catorce, enter the desert and guide *peyoteros*, and then these *peyoteros* followed him back to my place and told me of his wondrous deeds. Remarkable dog! I miss him so much!

Jimbo ate as much peyote as an ordinary *peyotero*, way more than your average person. Jimbo always tripped with me and ate mushrooms as well. He liked

Gerry in Wirikuta, 1999

to protect me on my treks, and became a good fighter capable of beating up to four ranch desert dogs at the same time. He was simply the best dog in Catorce.

Eymos and I ended up heading back to Estación Catorce, where we bought some mescaline gum (or cosmic bubble gum as I like to call it) and plunged into one of the most psychedelic trips of my life as we headed to the city of Real de Catorce. In my dream-like state, my visual perception of people allowed me to see their "animal" within clearly. Some were rats, others birds, others were creatures I dared not know. "Fear and Loathing in Real de Catorce."

Many friends visited me at my place in Los Catorce. We had magical times and guided many people to their spiritual and mental cure through the magic of peyote.

Building your home at age sixteen or seventeen makes you grow older faster. It gives you the power to quiet down your mind and have a bit of control over your destiny in a more mature way than any boy my age. I developed a character (shamanic) inspired by Carlos Castaneda, Huxley, and Eliphas Levi as I became a peyote guide.

I was way beyond my years exploring the deep realms of the mind by ingesting this sacred, most bitter cactus, hoping to clear my vision, my mission... my dream.

I lived a freedom I had never experienced before. My dear Jimbo and I started to explore the area. We now had a home of our own, and I began my shamanic training living by myself in the desert mountains of Real de Catorce. I learned about the *Brugmasia* magic flower for anxiety, the *Ariocarpus* cacti (locally known as "*chautle*") that if smoked worked as an antidote for a "bad peyote trip," and many other medicinal desert plants.

I had managed to walk through the desert with a plain pair of sandals, and had become a master at not getting stung by thorns in spiny Wirikuta.

Gerry hugging Natividad, aka "El Sar" from the Nahuatl community of Maruata, and on his left, Aldo from Italy (RIP) returning from a long trek in Wirikuta

I read about power plants, shamanism, and everything there was to know regarding the peyote cactus.

One of the many tales I like to tell is of my experience with a living intelligent light source locally known as *brujas* ("witches"). The local folk believe that witches had been living in their area for a considerable time and frequently visited the small villages at night in the shape of a burning fireball bouncing through the mountains jumping long distances, and supposedly feeding on the blood of newborns.

Apparently, they suck the newborn's blood out until it runs dry. There is a local saying that one must never leave a baby by an open window, because a witch will surely take it. Obviously, I was skeptical about it, and it was not until one night I was visited by something for which I still have no scientific explanation.

It was a warm summer night and I was sleeping on my hammock outside my home, when suddenly something woke me up. I checked the time; it was around three a.m.

I had managed to know the time by looking at the stars or moon.

I just opened my eyes from a nice comfy sleep. I looked around and saw nothing. I heard nothing. Something made me look across the river into a small hill right in front of my property.

All of a sudden a fireball jumped from behind the hill and started bouncing slowly but surely, six or seven feet from the ground. It just kept bouncing, not moving anywhere in particular. I screamed a loud "Wow! What is that?" It started to bounce slowly toward me! Like it knew where I was. I rubbed my eyes; it was still there. I yelled "*Una bruja!*" ("A witch!"). "Help!" I screamed. Then just before crossing the river the fireball stopped. It continued to bounce but didn't move forward, and suddenly it shone so brightly and then disappeared. I still have no clue what it was and I am pretty sure it was not a witch.

At least not my preconception of a witch — a woman who flies with a broom or conjures and makes spells, owns a black cat, etc. — but rather an intelligent, possibly alien entity that dwells in the mountains and possesses unique capacities such as flying and jumping long distances and telepathic communication.

The next morning half the town came to my house. Apparently, they all heard my screaming and hollering. I explained to them what I saw and they simply smiled and told me in a relaxed way it was "just" a witch. If you ask me it felt *alien*, like some sort of Close Encounter.

On the brighter side of living in Wirikuta was the wonderful opportunity to meet many Huichols. I had the honor to walk with them and to be accepted by a family that kindly named me "*Tu-Tun-Mah-Ne-Ka-nee-Ka*" (literal translation: "mountain dancing flower"). They were surprised how fast I walked. I loved to walk a fast pace. I tried to open my leg span as much as I could. They taught me species of cacti whose juices one can drink while thirsty in the desert, and certain fruits of cacti.

The distance between two points in Wirikuta by foot was quite long, so I learned to take as few steps as needed. I walked faster than a burro/donkey or mule. Locals and the mother of my firstborn liked to call me *huarache loco* or "crazy sandal." Beautiful times in the desert. And slowly but surely I started to decode *hikuri*'s (peyote's) message.

I was fulfilling my dreams. I was shown majestic visions, so much sacred geometry and cosmic knowledge! It told me I was a king! And of course it meant I had... a queen!

I found out by age eighteen that my ultimate goal was to find the woman of my dreams.

And since I was being such a good, well-behaved boy I was going to get my reward. Leaving home at such an early age, building my house, finding my life's purpose, and eventually finding the woman of my dreams were among the many blessings in my extraordinary life.

On one of the many adventures in the desert I found myself returning from a magical experience with my Jimbo. As we were walking the main trail back to Estación Catorce I saw a group of people walking toward the desert, about to cross our paths. I immediately focused on the most beautiful girl I had ever seen in my whole life, a blond, blue-eyed Argentinean walking with her buddies to Wirikuta. Our eyes met up and connected. She smiled at me. I returned an insecure smile back and saw how she walked into Wirikuta. After a while she looked back at me! She looked back!

"There is always hope!" the elf-queen says.

Thank God a couple of hours later, she and her friends arrived at Jefa Margarita's place right across from my room. I stepped outside and sat at the common concrete bench. She joined me and we introduced ourselves. Her name was Luz ("Light"!), she was from Buenos Aires, and her folks had recently bought a property on the coast of Oaxaca in the only presidentially declared nude beach in Mexico, Zipolite.

I immediately felt déjà vu and a jolt of light went down my spine, knowing in every cell in my body that she was the One. All my life in pursuit of the Light, the knowledge, and now the Universe/God had materialized in human form to love me in the name of Luz. She was my first true love. We had beautiful, innocent times. She stayed for two months, and before she took the train back to Oaxaca she told me to catch up with her there. I had found the Light of my life. It was time to go to Oaxaca not only for Luz, but to go to the famous place where the sacred, most powerful mushroom resided... Oaxaca!

I must say I was blessed to have had the opportunity to travel by train in Mexico. It was such a wonderful, unique experience. The trip from Estación Catorce to Oaxaca meant going to the capital, Mexico City, and taking another train down to Oaxaca.

A curious experience to see people getting on the train at every station offering their products. There were only two passenger train personnel: the ticket guy and a guy who sold peanuts, cans of soda, and cigarettes to all passengers. They always sat together either in front of the train or at the back, leaving an empty place to go and smoke some *wacky-tabacky*.

We traveled all the way to the station nearest to Huautla de Jimenez, called Teotitlan del Camino, on the hot sunny hot morning of June 25, 1997. I was in search of the sacred magic mushroom, at the famous place where Maria Sabina gave the magic shrooms to famous figures like Jim Morrison, The Beatles, and many others. I had brought with me a couple of rooted peyotes as a souvenir.

After getting to Huautla I was attended by a young woman who claimed she was the niece of Ma Julia, the actual Maria Sabina or mushroom priestess. She had a place where I could stay for an accessible price. As soon as I got there Ma Julia came to welcome me and told me to give her the thing I had brought her (the peyote) (how did she know?). I gave them both and she gave me my shrooms and advised me to eat all of them — she had added an extra dose for me, for I was, according to her, a strong tripper.

She gave me a wonderful *velada* or night ceremony, chanted mazatec songs, offered cocoa beans, and burned "copal" incense. When the shrooms kicked in, I listened to the chants while they showed me the magic of the sacred mushroom that manifested itself to me in a vision; it was just a glimpse of what was waiting for me. It whispered to me through my own feelings that I was going to have a special, extraordinary experience, but not there, not in Huautla.

So I decided to go to the capital of Oaxaca, a beautiful colonial city famous for its markets, churches, exotic gastronomy, dozens of different indigenous tribes, and for being the communal spot where all the seven regions would have a common trading place. A city with colonial architecture where some streets are filled with exotic aromas, such as Hidalgo Street, which pours into the atmosphere huge amounts of chocolate scent (every day thousands of kilos of roasted cocoa beans are milled in the street) that fills the road as you walk it. A great place to go is the Casa del Mezcal and have a mezcal shot with a twist of orange or lime filed with ant-salt (in Oaxaca locals grind a peculiar species of ant that dries into red tasty salt).

I went to the main plaza to enjoy some fried grasshoppers (the Indians love to offer fried grasshoppers to tourists; they are a bit salty but delicious), and was enjoying a great local coffee when this hippie girl came out of nowhere directly to my table and asked me if I had gone already to San José. I told her I hadn't. She got closer, gave me a big strong hug, and whispered to me, "It is waiting for you."

I finished my coffee and took the next available bus to San José. It was a third-class seat (if there even is such fare). A normal vehicle would make the trip in three hours, but our fifty-year-old bus took six to eight hours, stopping for every individual asking for a ride. I got to travel among peacocks and people holding large baskets of bread — I should have gotten paid for traveling like that. My patience was tested, and on the border of going nuts and just getting off the bus and taking any other means of transportation, I peeked out the window and saw a beautiful place filled with pine forests and musk everywhere, the clouds making a fascinating show. "Where is this place?" I asked myself. Suddenly I heard the bus driver yell, "San José Pacifico!" "This is it!" I thought.

SAN JOSÉ PACIFICO

L ocated over ten thousand feet above sea level in the Zapotec region, San José Pacifico is by far one of the most picturesque places in all Mexico. It was built on top of the southern Sierra Mountains, along the highway from Oaxaca to Puerto Angel on km 131,

Sunset from Gerry's ranch "Los Tzetziles" in San Jose Pacifico, Oaxaca

One of many beautiful sunsets
from a cabin in San José Pacifico

where under a sunny clear sky one can contemplate the Pacific Ocean. Famous for its mushrooms, edible and hallucinogenic, San José attracts people from all over the world who come to have the mushroom experience.

San José shelters dozens of species of pine trees, making a unique ecosystem. Always surrounded by clouds freshly formed in the ocean, San José is a beautiful, nature-filled place with excellent gastronomic fare, tasty coffee, and freshly made "pan Serrano"(wheat-based bread made with anise seeds). One can rent a cabin with or without a private bathroom or chimney.

As soon as I arrived at San José I was approached by a man who very politely invited us to his cabins, for only twenty pesos a night. As I was unpacking my stuff he offered us mushrooms. I asked for enough for ten trips. He was surprised but I assured him that I had already eaten some in Huautla and wanted to have a stronger experience.

"Our shrooms are stronger, the Mazatecs have chopped down their forests and the entity of the sacred mushroom has abandoned them, it dwells now in our forests," he proudly replied.

I stayed at Cabanas Pacifico and met Tia Ofelia Pinacho and Tio Leonardo Cruz, the main characters in the sacred mushroom sessions in this famous town. Eventually, I was "adopted" by them and lived at their house, played and shared with their children, Arturo (nineteen at the time), Heriberto (seventeen), and Uriel (seven), and actually ate magic shrooms with them. I had found my second family. They embraced and accepted me as their own and with time I was shown the sacred place where these wonderful fungi grow.

In San José there are only a few options: You can either have your shrooms fresh or in tea, during daylight in the forest or by nighttime in one's cabin. I went for the fresh option and decided to have them on an empty stomach one morning in the forest. I asked where I could go and was told that there are only two routes, uphill or downhill. Uphill on the top of Mt. Postema was a Zapotec archaeological site; a beautiful waterfall awaited downhill by the river.

Mt. Postema in San José Pacifico, Oaxaca, Mexico

I again took the first offer and started to climb uphill. I took the forest trail and found a pond in the middle of the forest; I chose to eat my fresh shrooms there. As I was focusing on the taste of them, a lightly acid-earth flavor, I began to realize my vision field started to manifest luminous fractals appearing and changing constantly in various tones of green, blue, yellow, and orange. I ate twenty-five landslide shrooms or *derrumbes*. Normally, an ordinary person would need seven *derrumbes* to have a magical experience. I was way out of my league.

Someone mentioned my Indian name should be "Two Roads" as I always encounter two opposite roads in every step I make. A friend from my childhood days from Guadalajara, Mario Cuevas, dedicated his life to the study of astrology and astronomy. Master Mario made me a very detailed astrological chart of my birthday and on it he had drawn a two-road pattern. He mentioned that my life would always demand I make choices, a decision between two opposite roads. I had to choose wisely.

THE ENTHEOGENIC EXPERIENCE

Entheogen ("substance capable of generating God within") is an ethnographic term used to describe a plant or drug that invokes a sense of the numinous or mystical experience. While several other well-known compounds — such as DMT, psilocybin, mescaline, and LSD — are often included in this category, James Oroc, Martin W. Ball, and I have personally found 5-MeO-DMT to be unique in that it is the only compound that has allowed us to experience an out-of-body reality that is both convincing and completely unlike any "known" reality. Other compounds such as DMT, ketamine, *Salvia divinorum*, and DIPT also have considerable reputations for producing out-of-body realities.

So there I was lying in the forest marching toward my own death by an overdose of the strongest mushrooms on Earth. I started feeling a strong presence in the woods; I knew something waited for me on the top of the mountain. A magical enchanted forest grows on Mt. Postema. The vegetation is a blend of misty forests and musky surfaces on a foggy scenario; amazing ferns and pine trees of so many kinds all around.

I climbed as fast as I could before the amount of ingested shrooms prevented me from taking a step. I reached a clear spot on what looked like the summit, but I saw a small hill like an underground pyramid covered in pine trees. I tossed myself to the ground and saw the clouds manifesting snakelike patterns with magical colors of purple, blue, and green.

I saw Aztec symbols everywhere I looked. Now I understood why my ancestors painted such images. Suddenly the clouds opened up and the sun (looking just like the Aztecs painted the sun — like the Sun Rock

Teonanacatl: Flesh of the Gods (Nahuatl tongue)

in Tenochtitlan or the ten-peso coin) emerged shining over me. I sensed all my energy being sucked like a UFO beam going toward the sun. I tried to grab on to myself, it was just too much! I thought I was losing my mind; I felt I was dying, I died! It was definitely too much juice.

I had eaten myself to insanity. I heard a voice within saying, "You ate too much, this is no joke, this is very scary. Who do you think you are?" I fell on my knees and started to cry and regret ever having eaten so many mushrooms.

I tried to induce vomiting but hopelessly I feared it was too late and all I could do was surrender to the experience. "*Hold on, man...* grab on to yourself," I told myself, as I saw how all my energy was swallowed by the sun and then I expanded in all possible directions.

I was the beginning and the end, the alpha and the omega, I traveled to the edges of the universe upon thought, there was no time, no space... I was eternity! I was God? Or God was me? I felt the divine self of our soul, our divine nature, I saw the Light of Consciousness, the Light of all living beings. I was in total awe. The only sound my body could try to make was a long continuous "*sssssssssssssssssssssssssssssssss.*"

I had defeated my greatest fear: death. And I was only eighteen years of age! What bliss! I never thought I was going to come back out of this experience; sadly for me I eventually descended to my baseline state.

I was in a constant, continuous state of awe over what I had just experienced. "No words," "They should have brought a poet!" as Jodie Foster said in the film *Contact*. I will never forget that magical July 25th of 1997.

The visions the sacred mushrooms have shown me I hold very sacred. Their nature is definitely divine. In other words, I saw God. I saw the force that creates everything in the universe. I could see the never-stopping ever-moving continuously changing energy force that dwells in every living being. I saw the Light! The Eternal Light of Everlasting Love that shines in our hearts.

The colors used by this mushroom are amazing tones of purple, blue, and green. Everything had an Aztec pattern: the sun, the trees, the rocks, my skin. The whole scope of my vision was Aztec patterns.

Now I understood our ancestors perfectly. Our ancestors were absolutely right in naming this mushroom *Teonanacatl*. It made perfect sense.

I was hooked on this substance, on this sacred *derrumbe* or landslide mushroom or Teonanacatl ("flesh of the gods" — the Aztecs gave the mushroom this name, indicating it was their most sacred substance). I stayed for a couple of months living in San José, ate shrooms every three days, and decided to head down to the beach, to Zipolite in search of my queen.

I had found one of the prettiest places on the planet. A wonderful forest lying on top of the Southern Sierra Mountains of Oaxaca, always covered in clouds and apparently ever-growing shrooms.

Enchanted Forest in Mt. Postema, San José Pacifico

The main town in the area is a Zapotec town called San Mateo Rio Hondo Yegoyoxi (most towns use their native name and a Spanish name), meaning "underground river." Back in the 1970s, the people of San Mateo heard the highway from Oaxaca to Puerto Angel was crossing their mountains and decided to build a small village along the highway that they called San José "Pueblo Nuevo" (New Town), or San José de las Flores, but the first teachers who arrived to educate them told them about the view and the possibility of gazing at the Pacific Ocean, so they changed the name to San José del Pacifico.

I decided to go to San Mateo and visit the nearby villages. I fell in love with those mountains. I still was in awe over my entheogenic experience with the *derrumbe* mushroom. I knew there was something about the ground, that the minerals made special the soil in which the mushroom grew.

I was told by the mushroom that the mycelium originates from thunder and lightning. Thunder gives off a sound at certain decibels at the same time that a drop of rainwater is being absorbed with the right amount of minerals, creating a magical spark. This gives origin to the mycelium that fruits these wonderful mushrooms. "Look at us, we are arrows pointing to our divine origin, we are always pointing upward to the heavens," they told me once.

These mountains are very special and the "cloud people" know it. They have managed to save part of their forests, thus enabling the mycelium to thrive.

There are so many shrooms that people from Huautla come to San José to buy mushrooms to fill their local demand.

There is a peculiar kind of landslide mushroom that grows gigantically. Locals refer to it as the Maestro or master. One is enough to trip three persons. I believe this is the Mexican *psylocybe azurescens* variety of these forests, being the strongest of them all.

Little Uriel Cruz Pinacho at age seven, deep inside a landslide taking Gerry on a sacred mushroom hunt, 1997

My new family from San José appreciated my fondness for their shrooms and usually saved the best Maestros or the best shrooms for me to eat.

As soon as I arrived at Zipolite I was told of the location of Luz's parents' house. After I waited a couple of hours she appeared, welcomed me, and gave me a huge hug. I tried to kiss her but she moved. She took my hand and we walked to the beach where to my surprise she dumped me.

She did not feel the same for me. Apparently she was about to take a journey with her brother to Guatemala and stay at least a month in Panajaxel, Lake Atitlan.

I was in shock, but before going into a depression I returned to San José to my second home with my new family to continue studying this wonderful medicine and learn as much from it as I could. I lived for a couple of months in this magical place.

Trekking up Mt. Postema and doing some research on the pyramid, I found some archaeological artifacts like broken copal or incense cups, and Alejo Porowi, a friend whom I took to see the place, found a turquoise eye.

I felt envy (shame on me) and returned afterward with greed. I started to dig many holes in an attempt to find something "larger" or more valuable, but just found many broken clay pieces.

I ate some Maestros and they made me pass through hell in a way that told me the sacred mountain must never be ravaged the way I tried to. How could I have dared to profane it with my silly, greedy thoughts? I was going to pay a high price for this.

My lack of respect for the place turned my experience into one of the most frightful trips in my entire life.

The mushroom told me that if I longed for Light so much, as punishment for my behavior I was going to get struck by lightning. I immediately felt the energy field and smelled the electricity in the air, then the clouds on top of me started to tremble and a strong lightning bolt struck a tree very close by. Jimbo ran immediately back to San José, leaving me by myself at the summit of the southern Sierra Mountains in the middle of a lightning storm.

"You wanted enlightenment, eh?" the mushroom joked. "Well, here it is!" and then another lightning bolt struck closer to me. I truly felt I was going to be struck by lightning yet KNEW that I was going to survive this punishment.

There was no point in running. "You can run but you can't hide," the mushroom told me.

I fell on my knees and began to pray. I asked for forgiveness. A couple more lightning bolts and more

Gerry and Uriel Cruz Pinacho mushroom hunting, 1997

thunder fell but this time, farther away. Slowly but surely, the heavens cleared out and the sun appeared. I was again stupefied. I went down to San José and into my cabin. The son of Tia Ofelia, Heriberto, came to visit me at my cabin and then another huge storm arrived with much thunder and lightning hitting close by; then the lights went out. I lit a candle and started to tell Heriberto of my mushroom trip. He listened to my tale very closely and when I finished, he stood up and told me I was a fool; that I was indeed very lucky for not getting struck by lightning. As soon as he said that, a loud thunderclap hit about a block from my cabin.

The mushroom always knows ways of hitting you where it hurts most. It is a very aggressive entheogen. But the reward after the punishment is a priceless bliss.

Having a good trip on *derrumbes* is one of the most enlightening experiences in my life. It is a true religious experience in itself.

The mushroom told me I had come to this world to heal people, to cure them... I was to become a doctor. I had to be humble and always remember all the experiences that I had lived. What is important in life is to "remember." To remember everything that has happened in order for us to evolve and not make the same mistakes, which eventually takes from us valuable priceless time, and hence Light.

Entrance to the enchanted forest in Mt. Postema, San Jose Pacifico, Oaxaca

These times in San José were some of the happiest in my life. After living for some years in the desert I felt like Tarzan set loose on this jungle-forest evergreen coniferous place filled with misty clouds every day. But now it was time to return to Babylon. It was time to enter college.

I had learned precious lessons from life. I had found my favorite place on the planet. I had found my direct line with the Source, or God (?) through this magical sacred mushroom.

People from San José know that the day I die I want my ashes buried beside my tree that lies at the summit of these mountains on Mt. Postema. I carved the word "gerry" on this tree, exactly on the summit of the Zapotec Sacred Mushroom Sanctuary.

I took a bus back to the desert for one more peyote trip, to say good-bye to Wirikuta, make some cosmic bubble gum for myself, and head to med school. I was going to miss Real de Catorce, my "high" school, my magical Wirikuta.

I enjoyed many nights watching the Hale-Bopp comet rise every sunset toward one of the most beautiful skies I had encountered.

Catorce had become my University of Life. I learned so much and for all those treks and trips, all those sunsets, all those teachings and everything I am so grateful.

During all those years living in Catorce I met very interesting people from the US, Italy, and Germany, and developed a good relationship with a buddy from Argentina called "Condor."

I invited him on this journey along with his buddy Willy, also from Argentina, who had just arrived to visit him.

The goal was to guide them to cross the Wirikuta desert and reach a famous place called Cerro de las Narices ("Nose Hills," basically a hill with rock formations resembling noses), where there is a hidden millenary cave with ancient cave paintings showing peyote trips and sacred geometry. This cave is close to the gold mine of San Carlos, one of the most treasured destinations in Wirikuta, which I discovered during my own explorations while I lived there.

This cave is also close to a valley where the peyote is among the strongest on the planet. It's notable for its whitish color, rather than blue-green.

I had learned during my peyote trips that peyote varies in colors ranging from a green, or blue or yellow, to even red or the rarest of them all, my favorite, which is purple. The difference lies in the concentration of mescaline. The least potent is green and the strongest is purple, although the most powerful of them all is the rare white peyote. It is considered to be a very special privilege to eat this.

Huichol legend tells about a white deer that dwelled in the Wirikuta desert and was the wisest of all deer. This applied to the peyote. Since the Huichol Indians also believe that the spirit of the peyote cactus, the blue deer or Tamatz Kaullamari, dwells in the Wirikuta desert and with each step makes a peyote grow, maybe there is an analogy related to the white deer and hence the white peyote; it was certainly true that if one eats a single white peyote one would trip for twenty-four hours. I must say that eating white peyote requires great human effort. As incredibly difficult it is to swallow normal peyote, you can imagine what was needed to swallow this one. Tears came out of my eyes when I did. Thanks to the white peyote, now I only need to see peyote, or even smell it, to get "connected" and alter my state of consciousness. It was one of the most difficult tasks I ever achieved.

There are many tourist attractions in Real de Catorce like horseback riding to the abandoned ghost town, visiting the Huichol sanctuary on the Quemado Mountain, going to the desert to eat peyote, visiting the mines, and a wonderful three-day trek to the mountains of the Catorce Sierra's forest in a magical place called Real de la Maroma.

Going to this cave with the millenary cave painting was the most secret attraction, reserved only for a select group of people. It took me years to get to this place and it was my trophy to be one of the few living in Catorce who actually knew the place.

So to say a good farewell to Real I decided to make this journey to the cave, then cross back over the desert and climb the mountains all the way to Real de la Maroma to the forests, and return through the mountain ridge summit back to Real de Catorce and eventually to Los Catorce, my home. A long but magical trek across magical Catorce or Wirikuta estimated to be done in a month or so of daily trekking.

THE LOST TREASURE

So we took off, leaving from my place after buying what was needed to walk for what I calculated to be twenty-one days. We managed to cross the Wirikuta desert and cut only the peyotes we were going to eat; any gram of weight added to our backpacks would eventually become very heavy.

I had learned to survive the desert heat with only a gallon of water per day, and traveled only with dried powdered corn or *pinole* as food. I rehydrated the *pinole* into a tortilla, added either salt or sugar, and ate it toasted on the fire coals.

So my peyote, a gallon jug of water, two pounds of *pinole*, my jacket, my machete, and my sleeping bag were the contents of my backpack.

We arrived after four days, walking all day long through the desert to reach the cave. We camped there for five days. I found a stash of *pedernal* rocks and *chuzos* (arrowheads) and my first green quartz crystal. I told Condor that I was going to go to the valley to hunt the "white deer" but I needed someone to stay at camp in case anybody passed by. Our food supplies needed to be taken care of.

So Condor told his buddy Willie to stay at our camp. We went down to the valley close by the largest dam in the area known as Presa de Santa Gertrudis to cut just three white peyotes, one for each. I decided to save this peyote for a special occasion.

We headed back across the Wirikuta desert and toward the Sierra de Catorce. It took another seven days to reach Real de la Maroma. During this entire trek we ate just one regular peyote per day, just enough to give us the pep or energy to thrive during the sunny day, resist drought and hunger, and limit our bodies to eating only at nightfall.

Gerry at age fifteen with two peyote buttons from Wirikuta

By the seventh day of eating one peyote per day we managed to get in touch with the peyote Spirit but without having strong visual hallucinations. I ended up sharing some morning glory seeds collected during my Oaxaca trip among my fellow companions, mixing the substances in an attempt to reach a more profound mystical state.

Once we headed back toward Real, I discovered a cave going deep into the ground. We decided to explore it.

We entered the deep underground realms, discovered halls full of crystals, stalagmites, and stalactites; we found many beautiful quartz crystals and other rock formations. We were in total ecstasy, our bags full of rocks and crystals as we gradually entered the bowels of the Earth, maybe a couple of miles. We saw the effect of light on certain crystals.

I believe we had gotten a bit greedy, taking as many crystals as we could, almost fighting for the largest or prettiest one, when suddenly one of our lamps went out. Condor panicked and ran to Willie, which made him more nervous, and left me to continue to guide the exploration. I realized we had to get out soon, so we turned back, leaving me on the back of the line following our buddy when suddenly he stopped and yelled, "No fucking way!" "What happened?" I asked him. "Closed wall, dead end, we are lost!"

We had managed to enter multiple deep halls inside the cave and now were clueless as to which was the one taking us out of there.

I am a bit claustrophobic and it hit me as soon as I thought about the idea of my battery lamp running out of juice. I took control of the tour and managed (thank God) to find the exit after two wrong choices. We eventually saw the light and followed it outside. For a moment there, we felt the fear of staying captured in the bowels of the Earth without ever coming out alive. I valued light! Sunlight!

So after crawling out of that hole we all drank more than we were supposed to. Heading back through the mountain ridge toward Real de Catorce we realized that we had run out of water. Night fell on us and we managed to take a different path downhill to the desert instead of going through the mountain ridge all the way to Real de Catorce. There was no moon over our heads to shine our path. We saw lights of a small town down in the desert, so we decided to get to this place to fill our water bottles, and climb back the next day.

The next morning, we realized we were in the small town down in the desert called Guadalupe del Carnicero, close to the railroad and surrounded by two small villages, San Antonio de Coronados and San José de Coronados.

San Antonio de Coronados, located southwest of Real de Catorce, has a profound history with deep roots in the formation of the Mexican Nation. While few documents relating how the events took place remain, a rich oral tradition conveys memories of what happened in these lands from generation to generation. It is thought that these lands were founded in 1620, having a second founding event in 1720. We know that the people who dwelled in this desert were nomads who would travel from one place to another in the region of the semi-desert plains of Wirikuta according to seasons. They would collect *cabuches*, *piñones*, and mesquite pods, and hunted maguey rats, quail, and, when in season, deer and wild boar. They respected the Earth, called her Mother Earth; they would celebrate her through the peyote ritual or *hikuri*. They lived in tribes and were very skilled with bow and arrow; we can still find their arrowheads in the hills. They were called Guachichiles, descendants of the Great Chichimecas. Later on, the Spanish conquistadors referred to them as *coyotes*, *borrados*, and *bozales*, among other slang names.

The violence imposed by Spanish conquistadors destroyed the Guachichil language but could not prevent tribes from visiting this place, where the Huichol

Indians come every year to honor and make offerings to the peyote cactus, and specifically visit the Ojo de Agua or natural water spring on the outskirts of Mt. Barco ("Mt. Ship") that nourishes and feeds life in San Antonio de Coronados.

The first Spanish conquistador who came here was Diego Coronado, under the command of Juan de Onate. For service given to the Spanish crown, mostly with violence and injustice, he was awarded these lands. The ancient grandfathers tell that he climbed Mt. Barco and asked for *merced* ("the favor granted by the crown") of all the lands he could see with his eyesight. So he was given the Sierra de Catorce (first known as Sierra del Astillero) and all the surrounding lands. He baptized these lands as Paraje del Coyote in reference to the nomads who dwelled there. He had three sons; one of them, Felipe Coronados, rebaptized the place and founded Ranchito de Coronados and San Antonio de los Coronados. Felipe Coronados died in 1754. He also was known for beginning a semi-imperial local way of governing the zone by *cabezas*. A *cabeza* was in charge of governing San Antonio de Coronados and this institution lasted until the mid-1800s. Then came the Mexican Independence, but injustice prevailed in these haciendas, until Porfirio Diaz in 1896 made "land titles" legal, dividing these lands among private entities. Then the Mexican Revolution began and a famous Otomi Indian called Guadalupe Alvarado led these lands during this turmoil. He managed to obtain military control over the government and was locally called Butcher Guadalupe or Guadalupe el Carnicero. A last battle was fought on a land formerly known as Guadalupe del Carnicero, also known as La Maroma.

After the Mexican Revolution people started to abandon the ancient way of living and eventually the haciendas, pursuing a dream of commerce and consumerism in the big cities. They left this place behind and it fell into ruins.

After having breakfast, Willie, Condor, and I decided to walk toward San Antonio de Coronados in search of peyote, to make some mescaline powder (dried and ground peyote). I pulled out my white peyote and ate it with so much effort, but finally managed to consume it completely. My stomach suffered a lot from this task — a high price for what could be achieved if one is lucky enough to be blessed with it. I personally think that eating this peyote was among the hardest tasks I have done. It was impressively bitter. As soon as it touched my tongue, my whole stomach contracted itself and I vomited. I managed with a lot of discipline and self-control to eat it and hold it for as long as necessary.

I had the most amazing, astounding, magical peyote experience of my life! I saw my whole life in a vision. I saw myself as a doctor, as a shaman, as a spiritual guide leading the people to the Light. I was ready to go to med school because the knowledge was *not* going to pop up in the sky and fall over my head, turning me into some self-made "messiah." I was a human baboon and had to learn all the evolutionary human mistakes made during the world wars that eventually produced giant leaps in the field of medicine.

To celebrate this precious knowledge, we snuck into an old, abandoned hacienda to smoke a joint. While we were having the "spliff" or *churro*, the place I was standing fell two feet underground, dropping me and scaring my friends.

They pulled me back on my feet and removed the broken pieces of wood. It was a secret compartment under the wooden floor. We saw a chest. You can imagine what we felt and what we thought... What an adventure! A treasure! Upon opening it we discovered the land titles of the hacienda and very old documents dating back to the eighteenth century! Documents from as early as the time before the state of San Luis Potosi was formed.

I had in my hands documents handwritten and signed by Coronado, grandson of the Spanish

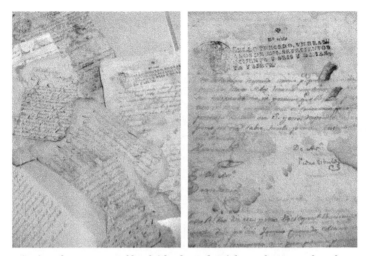

Ancient documents and land titles from the eighteenth century found at the Coronado Hacienda

Documents dating as far back as the 1700s

(left) Letter from the Coronado family
(right) A page from a personal journal, late nineteenth century

conquistador. Apparently this hacienda was built by his command, and was being managed by his family. Enclosed with the documents was a diary, his personal journal, his memoirs. To my surprise he used to worship Satan! I could read in his personal journal his invocations and prayers to the Dark Lord Satan. What a surprise for history.

My friends from Argentina thought it was rubbish. Maybe they didn't know who Coronado was. I told them since it was my finding I was going to keep them. They agreed and to this day they are among my most precious treasures. Eureka! I had done it! Now I was ready to head back to my parents' home in Guadalajara and become a doctor.

I went to the local phone booth in town and called my parents after almost three years of their not knowing a thing about me (at least that's what I thought). The only words that came out of my mind were, "Mom, I want to be a doctor, I want to enter med school, I learned my lesson." "Alleluia!" she cried! I was welcomed like the prodigal son of the Bible.

My education as a scientist, a medical officer, and a doctor took place. And that is my most valued treasure I have ever achieved, the knowledge and wisdom that no one can take away from me, my lost treasure.

MEDICAL SCHOOL

I returned to my hometown Guadalajara, in the capital of Jalisco. I entered the Universidad de Guadalajara at the medicine faculty of the Centro Universitario de Ciencias de la Salud, one of the most popular and important med schools in the country.

Med school was awesome. Learning how the body works was one of my favorite classes (physiology). Mycology, biochemistry, and herbolary were all sciences that I would later apply.

During my vacations I drove my jeep to the Huasteca Potosina, where famous prince Edward James, friend of Salvador Dali, bastard son of the king of England, found his paradise on Earth in the state of San Luis Potosi looking for orchids. I tripped on mescaline gum at the fountains of Edward James and entered mazes in the middle of the jungle, taking stairways leading nowhere. In the local jungle some

Gerry deep in the Mayan Jungle in 1999, close to Chichen Itza, uncovering one of the missing snake heads from the Castle of Chichen Itza

hallucinogenic shrooms grow as well so I could not waste the opportunity and mixed shrooms and cosmic bubble gum.

The jungle taught me so much. I realized that I could connect with Mother Nature in a way that resembles what is portrayed in the film *Avatar*. By linking to the Universal Grid of Consciousness, one can know which plants can heal you or are edible. Amazing natural knowledge can be acquired through the use of entheogens in the Huastecan jungle. While I stayed in the magical Huasteca Potosina I drank the mula-coffee drink composed of 3/4 coffee beans and 1/4 "mula" beans (large white beans that contain up to 5% pure caffeine, resulting in a significant boost in energy).

I also drove through the Mayan Peninsula, took the Ruins Trail, lived in Palenque for two months, picked my *Psylocybe cubensis* mushrooms on my way to the ruins, and shared experiences with all the hipsters camping at Mayabel, Pan Cha, or Chak. I lived a unique experience eating my shrooms prior to entering the Palenque Ruins, swimming in the Princess's river. I drove on LSD all through the Californian Peninsula, saw the gray whales and, on LSD, had close contact with one of them — a simply amazing connection between two living beings in Guerrero Negro. I discovered a beautiful beach along the Sea of Cortez called Mulege, in the middle of the desert but surrounded

Gerry and Jimbo at the Tajin ruins in the Huasteca Potosina

by date palms. I camped on the beach and the next morning the tide had moved about one hundred feet, uncovering hundreds of giant oysters. I went to get some lemons and some hot sauce and ate free seafood for two or three days.

I always identified myself with the spiral symbol; my name begins with a *G*, the natural spiral letter, the seventh letter of the alphabet. I always related to the number seven in my life. If you add together the numbers of my birthday (02/15/79), you get thirty-four; three plus four equals seven, my lucky number indeed. I was born in the house with the number 3031, again adding up to seven. Added together my driver's license and truck plate result in seven. I am fond of numerology and seven always follows me. Seven, seven, and again seven.

So when I lived in Real de Catorce I immediately identified a black rock fossil called ammonite, the first complex living being in the ocean, marked by rings in what used to be the Tethys Sea. I had found some large areas full of these ammonites. But I heard Charly talk of a place called Dr. Arroyo, located in the desert mountains as you drive toward Nuevo Leon state. This place is built around a mine of fossil ammonites. I located the place and drove with my dear Jimbo. There we found one of the most amazing fossil mines in Mexico. I remember

Gerry uncovering an ancient Zapotec cave in the forest 1999

giving the locals from this ranch a hundred dollars, and they gave me two large woven bags or *costales* full of fossils, weighing eighty pounds!

I went to Chiapas to trade the fossils and crystals I found in the cave for jade, amber, and fossil rock from the Mayan jungle. I lived for a month during my summer vacations in Palenque, and met very interesting folks from all over the world.

San Cristobal de las Casas, at the top of the mountains in Chiapas, is one of the most beautiful places in Mexico, where every Sunday all tribes come to the main plaza of Santo Domingo's church and you see hundreds of colorful *puestos*, places full of souvenirs, woven clothes, hippie clothes, so many colors, while all the Indians wear spotless white clothes. I had the best two-peso breakfast in the world, consisting of a glass of fresh *pozol* (cocoa beans with boiled corn and sugar and ice). With only five pesos one can have a delicious, full meal in the local *mercado* or market. At nights the plaza becomes a "poch" bar (a strong drink similar to tequila or mescal) where one can drink a cup of warm-fruit poch. Many locals spend the nights drunk on poch. I even saw Comandante Marcos up close and personal, when he entered the city with his men to give a speech.

One of the advantages of living in Guadalajara is its proximity to the Pacific coastline, only a two-hour drive. When I was young and having my first entheogenic and psychedelic experiences with Eymos and my gang, we discovered Maruata Beach, built in the Michoacan state by relatives of the ancient Aztecs who still speak their tongue. This beach is pre-Hispanic, in that everyone speaks Nahuatl (the Aztec tongue or dialect) and they made Mexicans feel foreign in their own country.

Maruata is part of a dozen tribe-towns belonging to the Nahuatl Indians in the regions of Michoacan and Guerrero. These Indians have not blended with the Mexicans and are very proud of their tongue. The government respects them. This coastline is known for its abundance of marijuana fields and a certain tolerance for smoking reefer. Everyone on the beach is smoking, even the little kids. Our own private legalize-it beach, and since the government doesn't stick their noses in Nahuatl Indian territory we can legalize pretty much anything in Maruata.

At least once a month I visited this beach and started to learn its dialect. I built a strong relationship with a family that is responsible for taking care of Maruata Viejo, a smaller beach just a few miles from Maruata. I loved camping in this place, and made many ceremonies with entheogens at this beach. Natividad was in charge of the beach so we became good friends, and he always shared his fish, lobster, any catch or hunt. Every time I went to Maruata, Natividad would welcome me with deer meat, lobsters, fresh fish, or whatever he planted and was harvesting. He had crops of peanuts, watermelon, and corn, among other delicious things. He always climbed a palm tree and cut plenty of coconuts for me to drink; he showed me many native edible plants and fruits. I was fascinated by their native tongue Nahuatl, which I started to learn, and wrote down my notes. We started to communicate in Nahuatl. He is a dear friend. I even took my Nahuatl friend Natividad from Maruata Viejo to Oaxaca to San

José, picked up Heriberto, and drove all three of us to my place in Real de Catorce. We had a wonderful time in Wirikuta. The people of Maruata are very thankful to me every time I visit them for taking one of their tribe on such an extraordinary trip. They take good care of me and for that I love them.

NEPAL AND INDIA

These were my young psychedelic tripping days. I graduated with honors and had the opportunity to spend four months in Nepal and India on a foreign exchange during my medical internship. People asked me where Nepal was and why out of the dozens of countries I picked Nepal. My reason was simple. I wanted to see mountains. The biggest and tallest of them all: Mt. Everest.

"Mountains, Gandalf, mountains! Hehehe!" I thought.

I wanted to see the Himalayan mountain range, see Sagarmatha (what the Tibetans call Mt. Everest) with my own eyes. Sadly, eight out of ten Mexicans can't identify the whereabouts of Nepal. And ten out of ten Nepalese are clueless as to where Mexico is on the globe. So during my medical internship at the City Hospital of Guadalajara I flew across the globe to encounter

Dr. Gerry trekking the Himalayas, Annapurna Base Camp, Nepal 2004

mystical cultures of the East, trekking the Kingdom of Nepal and India's Uttar Pradesh (or Northern States).

The trip was amazing. I flew to Atlanta, then to London, then by Gulf Air to Abu Dhabi in the United Arab Emirates. I arrived at an incredible golden dome in the middle of the desert by the Persian Gulf, gazing upon skyscrapers in the middle of the ocean by the Arabian desert, looking at oil sheiks at the airport with their wives wearing golden masks! This was simply an extraordinary change from the Western world I knew. I learned the high value of the dirham coin, and finally flew to mystical Kathmandu, capital of the Kingdom of Nepal.

To my surprise as soon as I arrived at Nepal I was told at the airport that they were in a chaotic phase, for the prince had murdered the king and queen (his parents) one week prior to my arrival and then managed to commit suicide, leaving the "uncle" on the throne, triggering a revolutionary movement rising against the "uncle." It was crazy times in Nepal, but coming from so far away I had no choice but to sign a "voluntary staying petition" at the airport.

During my trekking I arrived in places where the rebels had passed the day before and had raped the women and looted the villages. I was very lucky not to have encountered them during my stay in Nepal.

Dr. Gerry at Kathmandu Medical Faculty, Nepal 2004

My younger sister was living in London at that time and I went to visit her before and after my trip to Nepal.

Upon my arrival in Kathmandu I was received at the airport by my medical student exchange officer, Dipesh Pandey. His name means "King of Light." After I stayed in Thamel for a week, he invited me to stay at his parents' place to live the "traditional Nepalese way." I thank the Pandey family for all their attention and hospitality. They offered me a slave to carry my stuff around and take care of me. A slave!

As a Mexican I was not familiar with this kind of social interaction. So we became very good friends even though I never managed to get Ram to call me anything other than "Master." His name was actually Ramalaya but I kindly called him "Ram," or even "Rambo."

I had brought with me a couple of bottles of tequila, and that first night at the Pandey mansion we spent the whole evening drinking tequila shots and playing Uno (a game not known in these lands). Dipesh and Ram looked like little kids fascinated by playing Uno and drinking tequila. The next morning my slave had prepared chai tea for me. Every day during my stay, as soon as I opened my eyes Ram would welcome me, give me his blessings, and offer me my warm chai tea and some cookies. He took care of my clothes, carrying my stuff and being on the lookout for me. I told him every time not to call me "Master" and offered him my sincere friendship, some Western clothes, and money for his family — gifts he refused proudly. I was amazed.

While I lived in Nepal I realized that many people thought I was actually from Nepal; my dark skin gave the impression I was Nepalese. Locals are exempt from paying fees at many tourist attractions. So Dipesh thought it was a good idea to get false Nepalese ID papers. I became his brother "Deepak" (a name picked by him of course), a Hindu name meaning "god of light." *Funny!* I thought.

As I pursued the Light of Knowledge, light was always managing to manifest itself everywhere I went. Was it coincidence? Was it destiny? So the god of light and the king of light were off to trek around the kingdom of Nepal with our friendly slave, Ram.

I feel so lucky to have had the opportunity to live in Nepal. It was an amazing experience. Staying at Kathmandu and living in Thamel was an adventure I will never forget. Drinking chai tea, listening to "Om Mane Padme Hum" everywhere, learning the meaning of "namaste." I had the chance to go to Lumbini, the birthplace of Buddha, and the Chitwan Jungle National Park. I rode an elephant through the jungle, saw tigers and

Dr. Gerry coming out of a Forbidden Temple in Nepal

white rhinos. It was a one-of-a-kind trip of a lifetime for a guy coming from third-world Mexico.

I learned Nepalese jungle songs and heard stories of people having psychedelic experiences with elephant dung mushrooms! I visited ancient temples and sacred sites of the Eastern philosophies of Hinduism and Buddhism that no ordinary citizen of the Western world would enter. Fascinating cultures to admire coming from the Wild West.

I saw Mt. Everest with my own eyes. It was a majestic experience.

As long as I didn't open my mouth everyone thought I was Nepalese. I learned some ayurvedic medicine and was fascinated to learn that Shakira — the pop star from Colombia — and I both arrived at the Annapurna Base Camp the same day.

After my trip in Nepal and India I returned to London to stay at my sister's flat for a week. She took me sightseeing and we went to Camden Town. This place captured my attention because one could buy any drug there, legal or illegal. I saw magic mushrooms from Thailand and many exotic things such as *Salvia divinorum* extracts, Kratrom from Thailand and Indonesia, THC lollipops, and many items not ordinarily available on the streets of Mexico. I was surprised to see salvia extracts on sale. I had read about it and saw a native plant in Oaxaca at Ma Julia's house. But this was a salvia extraction of 60x!

So I decided to try this entheogenic substance coming from a Mexican plant at my sister's flat. It had a large red legend on the back of the vial that read something like: "Do not smoke this on your own!" I laughed. What could go wrong? I am Mexican!

THE SALVIA EXPERIMENT

I took a pinch of the whitish powder (pure crystals of salvia extract), placed it in a color-changing glass pipe, and torched it. After taking the hit I felt very odd. All my awareness shone as if an electric current were passing through it. My vision collapsed into something like millions of shards of glass shattering everywhere.

"I lost it!" I thought. I had lost my mind and for good this time. I must say that the salvia visions are among the most bizarrely dark and the weirdest of them all. Not a comfortable place to be. I saw how humans work as robots on the planet to fulfill the desire of a reptile that was always watching us. I freaked out so much! After coming out of it I was stupefied by the power of the experience and decided to keep more for further explorations.

In a way, I was preparing my body for all the subsequent entheogenic experiences of my life. It all made sense. I had to cleanse my body and mind with the peyote and learn its teachings in order to have my sacred encounter with the flesh of God through the magic landslide mushroom. Now I was appreciating life through the lens of the mystical *Salvia divinorum*. So much Light!

After returning from Nepal and finishing med school, I decided to perform salvia sessions in Guadalajara, starting with my friends and relatives. I eventually was introduced to many people curious to have the experience. I met many interesting persons, such as artists, writers, and psychologists, among other famous people from the Mexican upper class. At the time, a friend of a friend was selling the best quality LSD from Europe. He called me one day and told me he wanted to exchange entheogens. I agreed and he added that he had VIP passes for the GMS 3D rave party the following weekend. "Hell yeah!" I agreed.

Just after entering the party scene he pulled out some Gatorade and told me to drink it, that it had magic. I drank half and passed it along to him. I thought a good dose of pure LSD was a great way to start this party.

Even though I had dropped acid hundreds of times before, this time it felt different. I felt a huge pull of my hair through my scalp. I started to hear a light humming sound growing in intensity, just minutes after I drank the unforgettable Gatorade.

Little did I know that I was about to have the most potent LSD experience of my life. The evildoer placed 2500 mics of LSD in the drink!

I immediately saw cosmic light coming from everyone; my mind was manifesting itself and my thoughts everywhere! I sat down and put my body in the lotus position to meditate in this powerful state of awareness.

I immediately smelled incense of Tibetan temples and saw myself meditating and singing holy mantras with the monks. I saw the Himalayas again! Then I was in the VIP lounge having a drink with two girls coked up to their asses. I remember being asked by them who the fuck I was. I was in awe! My will was unconditional.

Then I was out of the party trying to find my car in the parking lot! All the cars were multicolored and constantly changing shape, and it took me hours to locate it. It was almost impossible for me to think, not to mention drive safely. I don't have a clue how I got to my parents' home but I remember this odyssey as one of the most powerful entheogenic experiences of my life.

So after med school I needed to go to San José to begin my life as their doctor, the magic mushroom doctor, in magical San José Pacifico.

Upon arriving at San José I sold my jeep and bought the summit of the southern Sierra Mountain ridge, the tallest private piece of land neighboring the enchanted forest. This place is locally known as "Rancho Los Tzetziles." The view from my land is amazing. At night one could see the lights of ships cruising the Pacific Ocean and the lights of Puerto Escondido.

Living in this magical place I learned applied mycology and was taught over eighty species of edible mushrooms; I was also shown the spot where the sacred mushroom resides. Europeans taught me how to make butane bubble hash or dabs. I was having the time of my life.

I learned that the Zapotec Indians of the region long ago had built a pyramid on top of this mountain (Mt. La Postema, the tallest peak in San José) to honor their gods, and specifically to honor the mushroom deity. This pyramid now was covered with forest, trees growing on top of it. This place was their sanctuary, their holy place where the mushrooms reside.

Living in San José Pacifico as their medical officer was a true honor, my dream come true. I could not have been happier.

Every day I woke up, had a tasty coffee, and just immersed myself in the woods. I always returned with kilos of edible mushrooms, even six-pound mushroom specimens like *Bolletus*. I dried some shrooms for selling and also learned how to cook them. I definitely developed and applied my mycology knowledge.

The *derrumbe* mushroom told me so many things about the forests. It told me how to create a fire in the middle of a thunderstorm (if you slice and cut a root of any pine tree, it will burn no matter how wet it is), and to my surprise it showed me at least a dozen edible mushrooms. I cannot explain it; only people who have eaten this mushroom can understand how it "talks" to each and every one of us.

This mushroom has the capacity to punish us if needed or reward us. It is the fastest and most guaranteed divine justice applied to an individual.

Many people speak of the wonders of this entheogen. I heard stories of brain tumors disappearing over a mushroom trip. A patient of mine told me that her headache, which no medicine could relieve, was cured

Dr. Gerry and Jimbo in the African-slave-descendant community of Chacahua in Oaxaca, Mexico

through the mushrooms. One day she dreamed of eating mushrooms and on her way to the mill she found a "family" of *derrumbes*, which she ate on an empty stomach. During her trip the mushroom told her what she needed to know and that was the last headache of her life. No, she did not die. She is alive and well and living in San José Pacifico.

Mushrooms offer by far one of the most magical spiritual experiences. Through them, nature is either kind enough or cruel enough to show us what we have done with our life and has the capacity to show us the "future," or events that will manifest if one continues to live the same way. It's an evolutionary tool toward achieving the ultimate way of living: consciously.

THE FALL INTO THE PIT

There is no way of differentiating heaven from hell unless one gets as low as possible. Only by encountering one's own darkness, can one truly recognize the light and heaven. I was no exception.

After Nepal a series of events led to the fall into my own abyss. My mother was diagnosed with breast cancer and underwent a total radical mastectomy, radiation, and chemo. It was a strong blow to my heart.

At the same time my girlfriend after two magical years dumped me for being fond of entheogens (the main reason why every girl dumps me). My daughter was born and I was not there. Jimbo died with open eyes and again I was not there, and I crashed my truck. Talk about rough times.

I thought it was not fair that those things could happen to me. I went into a depression and fell into the claws of a horrible addiction to one of the most addictive substances in the world: crack.

I lost everything. My family, my friends, my life, my dog, my truck, my girlfriend, my child! It was not until I touched the bottom of my own pit that I realized my true destiny and stood up from the lowest place I reached. By using my own medicine (5-MeO-DMT) I was able to surmount such a horrible nightmare and disease. It cost me years, money, and eventually precious time.

During this time, I hardly consumed entheogens. I was mad at God in a childish way. Even though I kept witnessing the medicinal properties of entheogens I maintained a distance with an angry attitude toward life in general, until divine intervention fulfilled its task.

God works in mysterious ways.

While I lived in San José I secretly suffered from anxiety attacks related to my crack addiction. When I finally had a sacred mushroom ceremony and asked the medicine for help, the shrooms told me there is always hope and a sacred Light was going to reach me soon.

Within a few days a friend of mine living in San Mateo Rio Hondo, the head municipal town of the region, offered me a DMT experience. A friend of his from Australia had extracted DMT from an acacia tree. I will never forget the first time I smoked DMT.

Just like Terence McKenna's trip, I was launched into a fascinating colorful world. My mind was blown in just one puff. I could not believe just one puff had the power of dozens of landslide mushrooms or dozens of peyote.

It was during the following week that two hippie-looking guys from the US came to my attention. They were offering DMT sessions for only one hundred pesos (less than ten bucks) around San José Pacifico. God bless these two men.

I had my first 5-MeO-DMT experience on top of the mountains on my land, a beautiful setting surrounded by clouds. I felt an enormous healing power come over my body. My whole self melted in yellow golden and pinkish patterns of spirals, a colorful,

Dr. Gerry and Dr. Rettig arriving from first toad milking, 2006

delightful experience. I saw the Universal Grid of Consciousness! I made peace with God. I was face-to-face with the Ultimate Source.

This was the beginning of my new life, the end of my rehab. I had found the substance capable of changing the world in which we live! Eureka!

We spent several months sharing DMT and LSD and I took them to meet the sacred mushroom mycelium that was entrusted by the local Zapotecs. Very sacred places where the *derrumbe* grows. Eventually they told me the secret of their DMT source. To my surprise it was toad venom, from the Sonoran Desert toad.

I knew I had to do something with this wonderful medicine. I studied everything I could about 5-MeO-DMT, called my colleague, fellow follower of entheogens and good friend Octavio Rettig, and together we took our first quest in search of the Sonoran Desert toad, the mythical *Bufo alvarius*.

Dr. Gerry and the Sonoran Desert toad

I had found the Source!

Thanks to the entheogenic capacity of 5-MeO-DMT it was possible for me to cure my soul and my mind and body from that horrible addiction, and realize the true meaning of my life.

I learned to love and respect myself as a primary requisite for loving someone else. I had found God in me; I had felt his "grace" (sorry for the Catholic terms) and learned how to properly administer this sacred "venom" to other people. I had found my medicine, The Medicine.

After a psychedelic trip into the Sonoran Desert with a bit of good LSD magic, I arrived at the secret toad site in the Sonoran Desert whose location I was entrusted with back in San José. There were hundreds of toads; it felt magical to be among such brave toads.

The heat from the Sonoran Desert made it impossible to be outdoors during daytime. The environment is too hostile for an amphibian dependent on a continuous water supply.

Amazingly these toads can stand the infernal heat by staying underground and coming out only at night. I learned that this magnificent being spends nine months of the year deeply hibernating underground in a coma-like state, waiting for the thunder to wake him up (thunder and lightning being condensed light and sound). Only during the monsoon season in the Sonoran Desert (a two- to three-month period) does this toad wake up to eat, reproduce, and also die when attacked by predators. This was amazing stuff.

I began performing 5-MeO-DMT sessions around my country, and went to Europe every once in a while to share this medicine, my experiences, and the testimonies of over nine hundred people who have actively participated in a ceremony of a lifetime.

I was a spark that became part of the movement that shared this medicine with the local Indian tribes of the Sonoran Desert. I was surprised they were not aware of the medicinal, magical, entheogenic properties. They still used the peyote in their rituals. Nomadic tribes not supported by the local or federal Mexican government suffered modernity's mistakes and sins. Many young members of the Seri or Yaqui tribe had fallen in the claws of crystal-meth addiction. This was

Dr. Octavio Rettig and Dr. Gerry back in 2007 and toad milking in 2014

a perfect moment to test the medicine's capacity for a hard-drug rehab treatment.

My friend and colleague Dr. Octavio Rettig had been studying drug addictions, and used himself as a test subject. He proved the medicinal healing properties of the amazing secretion of the *Bufo alvarius* toad on his crack addiction.

I introduced him into the world of entheogens, had taken him for his first time to Wirikuta, to San José Pacifico, and now to the Sonoran Desert. He went to the Seri Indian Headquarters at Punta Chueca in the state of Sonora, and began a project that demonstrated the healing properties of smoking toad venom for the treatment of addictions. He gave this sacrament to the Seri chief and with his blessing nowadays we both travel around the world as living witnesses of the magical healing properties this sacred secretion possesses.

It was this magical toad of wonder that had the solution to save humankind from the material-consuming society we live in... it was a toad, we had managed to kiss the toad and the Prince of the Sonoran Desert in return gave us a mission. It was the *Bufo alvarius* toad's secretion from the Sonoran Desert in my country, magical Mexico.

BUFO ALVARIUS
(INCILLIUS ALVARIUS):
THE SONORAN DESERT TOAD

These fascinating toads belong to the Animalia kingdom, Chordata Phylum, Class Amphibia, Order Anura, Family Bufonidae, Genus Incilius, Specie Incilius Alvarius. They roam in the Sonoran Desert, an area that runs 100,000 km from western Sonora, to northwestern Baja California, Mexico. And up through southwestern Arizona and southeastern California in the US.

These Batracius desert princes belong to the family of Bufonidae, amphibious beings composed of 485 species of bufo toads worldwide. *Bufo alvarius* is now known officially as *Incillius alvarius*, aka "The Colorado River Toad." And it has been a peculiar being that has passed unnoticed from humanity until recent times. It was not until the mid-sixties (around 1965) that 5 Methoxy DMT was discovered in the venom in its glands. The *Bufo alvarius* toad is the only creature in the world that is known to contain 5-MeO-DMT (the strongest entheogen known so far). The venom can contain up to 15 to 20% percent 5-MeO-DMT by volume when dried, depending on the number of times the glands have been milked, decreasing progressively and taking a whole year to concentrate it again. *Bufo alvarius* is semi-aquatic and needs a dependable water source to survive. To think that this living creature resides in one of the hottest and driest places on Earth. It has thrived, however.

The *Bufo alvarius* toad possesses a peculiar enzyme, O-methyl transferase, that changes by a process of methylation (adding a methyl or CH3 group at the fifth carbon position in the indole ring) the common bufotenin into 5-MeO-DMT. This unique creature is the only known true entheogen-producing animal

Bufo alvarius **toads, Sonoran Desert, 2006**

on Earth. This enzyme makes the medicine cross the blood-brain barrier faster and more potently than regular DMT. This chemical reaction occurs within the single-layer cell inner membrane that covers the glands of these toads. This 5-MeO-DMT accumulates in the toad's venom.

We can see the obvious relationship between toads and divinity. Many bufo depictions can be observed in the Mesoamerican civilizations of the Olmec, Mayan, and Aztec. It represents the cycle of fertility, the rain season, life coming from the ground. There are many toad depictions in Aztec, Mayan, and Olmec art. Large quantities of bufo toad skeletons have been found at Olmec ceremonial sites.

Bufo Pre-Hispanic art, circa 1000 AD

It is important to know that there are no *Bufo alvarius* outside the Sonoran Desert. The most predominant toads in Mexico are the large *Bufo marinus*, or cane toads, commonly dispersed through the Yucatan Peninsula and presumed to be the toads represented in Mesoamerican mythology.

Toad depiction at Pakal's Tomb at
Palenque, Chiapas

Toad depiction at
Cacaxtla caves in
Mexico Valley

How did these events happen? How did we end up milking toads? How did we get ahold of this ancient knowledge?

The shamans claim that the plants told them. That all can be known if you listen to the plants and your dreams.

> ... [T]here is no physical proof that the tribes of Meso-america knew that *Bufo alvarius* possesses venom that is psychoactive when smoked, there's some pertinent circumstantial speculation. From the wide diversity of entheogenic plants that these tribes used, it is clear that their shamans actively searched for such things, curiously experimenting with numerous natural substances, often at the risk of their own injury. According to Davis and Weil, "Many Indians regarded smoke as sacred essence, a vehicle to the spiritual world. The use of tobacco established a pattern of consuming psychoactive drugs by smoking.
>
> James Oroc, *Tryptamine Palace*

I have come to believe that the Indian tribes of the Sonoran Desert could not have identified *Bufo alvarius*

Toad art in Mayan codices

Tlaltecuhtl: The Aztec Earth Goddess

entheogen and traded it to their southern neighbors. I strongly believe the time for this entheogen is now and not before. The locals dwelled all the time with the toad, yet there is no evidence whatsoever that they used it. First of all, the toad medicine is only active when vaporized, not burnt. And for the maximum entheogenic effect of this medicine, a "torch lighter" is needed for a quick combustion. Any slower method of ignition will not release enough medicine and therefore won't produce the entheogenic experience needed. Neither of these two requirements was available in ancient times. And toad medicine is not active orally nor in any other way.

The time for this medicine is now; it is trying to bring us back to the path, back to experiencing the true knowledge of God.

Now I dedicate myself to spreading this message, these words, this Light acquired through entheogenic experiences in an attempt to create or start a spark of

Light in a reader or a participant in the 5-MeO-DMT ceremony, and make a difference in today's world and lifestyle. I want to try to reach, turn on, or enlighten as many people as possible, connecting them to the spiritual world, which, whether we like it or not, exists!

It is my humble pleasure to be part of this Light that slowly but surely is expanding throughout the globe.

Only through the means of an entheogenic experience can one truly realize the divine and sacred nature of our life and return to the Source or the point of origin. As I like to point out, life is but a huge and magical apocatastasis, "the return of things to the point of origin."

Funny to realize as I made a retrospective view of my life that "coincidentally" a Seri Indian guided me in the Wirikuta desert and taught me a Seri song that mentions the word *otac* ("toad" in Seri tongue) and became my power song for many years. I proudly sang it in temazcal ceremonies, ayahuasca ceremonies, and in my own 5-MeO-DMT ceremonies. It was a wonderful feeling to relate it years later as I encountered this magical molecule of the Sonoran Desert. Was it destiny?

I had learned a shamanic power song at age fifteen, and it was not until 2005 and 2006 that I realized its purpose when I met the Seris and learned the word *otac* or *boboc*. It all made sense in a strange way. Recalling the Seri chant taught in my younger years in Wirikuta — "*Haya haya OTAC* (toad!) *ferenze mare-vaya, ...*" — I felt again that this was no coincidence.

Toad medicine's psychedelic effects are believed to come from its efficacy at the 5-HT2A receptor as a partial agonist. Specifically, this molecule shows high affinity for the 5-HT2 and 5-HT1A subtypes. Additional mechanisms of action such as reuptake inhibition of neurotransmitters including serotonin, noradrenaline, and dopamine are also involved.

Additional studies of neuroscanning or neuroimaging and neuroanalysis like the QEEG/Bufo Project by Dr. Juan Acosta Urquidi (in which electrodes are placed on the scalp) revealed fascinating stuff, like the appearance of a huge theta wave (6 to 8 Hz) that emerged during the ASC (altered state of consciousness), after no theta peak was detected in baseline brain maps. It persisted 10 to 20 minutes after the intake of medicine. Complete recovery to baseline conditions occurred 20 to 30 minutes post-inhalation. Dr. Acosta also measured increased gamma power (38 to 40 Hz) during Bufo ASC, which persisted up to 20 minutes. This wave pattern behavior is also found during deep REM sleep. Upon neuroimaging a predominant increase in blood flow of the lymbic system, medulla, and pineal gland was also noted. Such studies are now being conducted by friends of mine and will be published soon.

The level of healing that 5-MeO-DMT produces in the individual is so deep, so real, so medicinal. The short- and long-term effects on human perception and its capacity for producing a pure entheogenic experience (experiencing God within ourselves) from a single exposure to this molecule — besides being amazing/ intense/terrifying — are always positive and engender no harm, no addiction. Instead, the toad medicine leaves a benign outcome for the individual who is able to surrender, let go, and just... reach liberation through direct experience of reality, with no ego-generated illusions of existence... with the clarity afforded by genuine self-knowledge.

THE TRANSFIGURATION

Alex Grey creates wonderful paintings showing the spiritual worlds or spiritual bodies. Two of many favorite paintings: *Dying* and *Transfiguration*. They are true masterpieces of art showing a medicine man who has to face all his demons and fears and undergo death and rebirth to rise toward the Light of Knowledge and then be able to teach humanity.

There is no better metaphor for explaining the experience of smoking toad venom than the masterpiece *Dying*.

This process of becoming one with the Source or God was a transfiguration. A process that began the day Wirikuta called and bestowed upon me the honor of living as an eighteen-year-old on the summit of the southern Sierra Mountains of San José Pacifico.

I found the purpose of my teachings and lessons, the ultimate knowledge, the Ultimate Truth, by smoking the vapors of these golden crystals of dried toad venom.

These are my greatest treasures, the goal of my adventures. Even though I walk my path alone in constant communication with the spiritual world, I will continue to spread this Light as long as possible.

It is of no surprise that just when mankind is far away from the spiritual world, submerged deep in materialistic labyrinths and artificial lights, that DMT, specifically 5-MeO-DMT, appears with a firm purpose: to awaken the individual to remember our divine origin. By reconnecting us with our true purpose, 5-MeO-DMT performs a noble apocatastasis.

We have to return to the Source, embrace this medicinal beautiful Light, and save what's left of our planet before it's too late.

I strongly believe this is what the Mayans predicted would happen in 2012: the release of 5-MeO-DMT worldwide, spreading spiritual Light to the planet, Light coming directly from the center of the galaxy and the center of the universe (or as I also like to call it from now on "multiverses").

Now is the time, here is the place to have this uniquely fascinating experience — a wonderful circumstance we live in.

We must learn to trust the universe and accept the life that was given to us. Once we achieve total acceptance, we can truly begin to live our life at its fullest with happiness and health.

It should be noted that different people experience different levels of entheogenic effect due to their own personal, intellectual, and spiritual development.

Those who are blessed by "kissing the toad" report it to be the most transformative event in their lives. They feel God's grace and become God. They experience a true mystical experience, called "non-duality" or a "non-dual state," or an entheogenic state; the condition described by Saint Paul as the "peace that transcends understanding." Depending on their belief system or theosophy, some call it Cosmic Consciousness, Zen, Satori, Muktha, Samadhi, Nirvana, Tao, Kensho, Objective Consciousness, or Internal Light.

All these terms describe a self-transforming perception of the total union of the Self with infinity. It is beyond space or time, beyond words; it is non-temporality, eternity, unlimited unity with all the living universe. This state is characterized by the destruction of the Self by a new definition of the Self.

In this redefinition of the Self, "I" stands for all humanity, all life, and the whole universe. Ego as we know it transcends the body limits, ceases to exist, dies, and suddenly becomes one with everything that has always existed.

THE OUTCOME

After performing over 1,600 ceremonies (and still counting) for people from different parts of the globe, I have witnessed the magical healing properties of vaporized venom of *Bufo alvarius*. It can cure addictions, depression; I have seen with my own eyes the medicinal application for many illnesses that afflict mankind nowadays.

I have introduced this sacred medicine to doctors, lawyers, psychologists, therapists, my dad, old senile patients, artists, AIDS and cancer patients, severely depressed people, schizophrenic patients, and drug addicts. All sessions turned out with marvelous positive results.

It is the only substance I have witnessed capable of showing us who we really are. It removes our ego-made masks and shows us what we are made of... Light!

As a gynecologist, I haven't got the time to dedicate my life fully to this sacred molecule and spread the word of its value. But I am humbly proud of what I have done and realized. As an ob-gyn, I am a witness to the birth of humanity, but through this amazing spiritual work, I am also a witness to humanity's *re*birth.

I believe that the secretion of the *Bufo alvarius* toad was the magical component in the smoke blend used by the Sonoran Yaqui Don Juan Matus in Carlos Castaneda's book *The Teachings of Don Juan*, which he loved to call "*humito*" or "little smoke." Reading that Castaneda's experience of smoking *humito* was such a powerful entheogenic experience can only lead to the suspicion that it actually was 5-MeO-DMT from the Sonoran Desert toad; something that was kept secret for so long, escaping the Spanish conquistadores and the Inquisition that tried to abolish all signs of polytheistic religions.

Hollywood has also secretly tried to capture the magic and power of entheogens such as in the film *Renegade,* in which Mesoamerican Indians, my ancestors, gained the most sacred knowledge from their treasured entheogens.

One can only presume that everything is in place at the right time, with all happening for a reason. I am not so interested in the past use of this medicine but in the actual and future use of this powerful entheogen.

For some reason 5-MeO-DMT has appeared now. Let's accept it and embrace it like the Seri Indians have, giving it a proper use, with the respect it deserves.

I suggest preparing the body and the mind for the experience. In order to achieve the maximum knowledge or wisdom one would need to respect and have high intentions for the experience when ingesting an entheogen.

I must emphasize that I have never used an entheogen for entertainment purposes, except for LSD in common doses. All of the hundreds of experiences or trips I have made have had a purpose. My respect for the experience has always been as profound as it is for the substance. I act as a facilitator of the experience in a ceremonial setting.

The ceremonies are shared in a loving context and with mutual respect, with attention paid to what every person requires in their process of evolution. The sole purpose of these ceremonies is to reconnect the human being to the primary or primal Source. All people, regardless of their conditions or gender, may become masters of their own consciousness, and receive privileged access to perform an apocatastasis, returning to their own selves again by means of liberation, healing, purification, and transformation.

Since I was young living in Catorce I have always pursued knowledge to become a better man, to help my relations.

I have always consumed entheogens to attain a religious experience.

Entheogens are the fundamental pillars of my religion, of my relationship with God or the Source or the Light. So instead of going periodically to church or a temple I prefer to have a trip or an entheogenic experience.

I don't believe in partying with entheogens. If I used them a lot, it was probably because it was my destiny. Any other ordinary individual surely would have lost his or her mind.

Humans suffer from a disease I call "Everlasting Dissatisfaction Syndrome." We will never be satisfied with what we possess. It is our human desire to want more, be more, in an endless effort to fill a space that will never be filled with material things. Eventually we will end up like a spider trapped in its own web.

Overpopulation, waste, pollution, depletion, and destruction work synergistically to influence humankind in a negative way.

This human desire for overconsumption or *consumerism* is the main factor obscuring our purpose. Entheogens, I believe, are the cure for this evil human disease.

We must learn to love what we possess and be grateful with the life that is given to us.

There is a relationship between light exposure and endogenous (or naturally produced) DMT. The less exposed our brains are to artificial light, the more DMT will be pumped into the brain's bloodstream. Without this exposure, ancient Biblical characters such as Moses, Abraham, and Isaac had more DMT endogenously and hence were able to have such profound religious experiences. This explains the multiple revelations of divinity received by humankind in ancient times.

As soon as we created artificial light we deprived ourselves of secreting naturally produced DMT, and maybe 5-MeO-DMT, by the pineal gland. Technology basically separated us from the Light Source, the Divine Light of Consciousness. And that is why I believe now is the time for this medicine to be shared among our tribes worldwide. This might just be the solution we are all waiting for.

The Sonoran Seri Indians name all toads *otac*, the Yaqui Indians name the desert toads *boboc*, and the Mayans call all toads *Xpek*.

Amazed by it they embraced it and now besides using peyote, they use this sacrament in their ceremonies.

Now in my free time I share this molecule and medicine with the people along with my Seri chant and sacred mantras in a ceremonial setting based on respect and the will to be a better person.

I won't go deep into the testimonials of the individuals who have been a part of this quest, in order to respect their privacy, since many were drug addicts, or had severe mental issues or were living a nightmare, like myself. But just to mention some: women suffering from sexual repression, severely depressed people, victims of strong drug addictions, patients with terminal disease, families separated by madness and reunited by an entheogenic experience — these are a few of the many different circumstances that my dear and precious toads' secretion has cured and fixed. I have been following up on as many people as possible and have discovered there are definite pre- and post-states of awareness induced by 5-MeO-DMT or other entheogenic experiences.

I recall the experience of a well-known, very bright psychologist. As soon as the medicine entered his body he started to scream, "It burns! It burns!" He yelled uncontrollably. I tried my best to calm him down. Afterward he told me he had been sent to hell, and even breathing burned. It was the most horrifying experience of his life. He complained to me. He demanded an explanation for what I had "done to" him. It took him a long time to calm down. The last complaint came a month after his experience, when he called me asking the same question: "What the fuck did you give me, Doctor?"

But whether they have good or bad experiences from 5-MeO-DMT, everyone who tries it evolves in some way. They also contribute in fulfilling my dream-purpose of spreading this Light, curing and healing humanity.

We have a curious capacity to learn from an entheogenic experience. It is crucial to have time to assimilate it and have feedback regarding the experience.

Many can testify that the Truth has set them free.

It has now become more than a mission, a purpose to get together with the Light tribe and share this Light and fulfill the planet's will.

I have always seen positive results, short- and long-term, everywhere I give this medicine. It has really become more of an honor to be part of this enlightening movement, the Light Revolution of Consciousness.

Now that I have learned from my mistakes I can proudly show my scars. I embrace them and hope to become a better man every single day, conscious of the spiritual world and of every word put into action — thanks to the magical healing and enlightening properties of 5-MeO-DMT.

I am a manifestation of the Light that has come to awaken my brothers and remind them that we are all one. We are one living, conscious being. Our planet is alive and we are all connected to every single thing in the whole multiverse.

Hikuri cleaned my body, showed me the right way to live, *Teonanacatl* ("flesh of the gods") enlightened my mind, and the *Bufo alvarius* or "*sapito*" ("little toad") secretion turned on or reconnected my soul with the Divine Light to shine on and through myself, my kind, my offspring, and my planet.

All entheogens are *peyotl*, *hikuri*, or *jicuri*. All are God's Light... God's molecules.

We are beings of Light that decided to condense into matter through our human-bound form.

Now I only have to look back at my life and my actions to confirm I was destined to have a long spiritual path toward enlightenment. And thanks to these entheogens I have grown to be a righteous man with a rich spiritual life devoted to service.

All experiences have made me who I am today: Dr. DMT, Dr. Gerry Alvarius, even Dr. Bufo, or simply Dr. Gerry. Whatever people call me they constantly remind me of my purpose. I humbly accept the honor of delivering this sacred molecule to as many people as possible in my life's span.

● ● ●

After having my experiences with 5-MeO-DMT and returning from the Sonoran Desert, I decided to move to the Mexican Caribbean to start fresh in a beautiful paradise called Mahahual or Costa Maya.

Arriving close to the end of 2006, I eventually became the local doctor of the town that had a huge port where eight cruise ships would stop for a glimpse of a small, calm, Caribbean fishermen's town called Costa Maya. The main attraction is the Chinchorro Reef Barrier, located right in front of the beach, just a couple of nautical miles offshore. Being the second largest barrier reef on the planet has made this place a prime destination for divers and adventure seekers; the True Paradise on Earth of magical Mexico.

Shaman Chicho Novelo preparing the Sacred Bath Brew for a participant

The reason why I ended up there was because I wanted to be as close as possible to the DMT-containing plants found in the Central American snuffs of 5-MeO-DMT called yopo, epena, and vilca. I wanted to apply my chemistry and biochemistry knowledge and extract DMT from these plant sources.

A dear friend of mine, whom I had taken to the sacred mushroom ceremony in San José a couple of months earlier, came to Mahahual to visit me. His final destination on those holidays was an entheogenic ranch in Belize about an hour and a half from the Mexican border. On this famous ranch one could have an entheogenic experience with yopo snuff, ayahuasca, magic mushrooms, and Hawaiian baby woodrose seeds. I had to go to this place. "Entheogenic Ranch?" I asked. "*Sssssssss*," I hissed with a huge smile on my face.

Located south of Corozal at August Pine Ridge, the Hummingbird Ranch received psychedelic tourists

Dr. Gerry holding a *Anandanthera peregrina* (yopo tree) branch before entering medical residency

from everywhere. Famous writers and journalists have had the magical opportunity of staying at this ecological auto-sustainable forest of yopo trees (*Anandanthera peregrina*) planted by the shaman Edmund some forty years ago. He brought the seeds from a tribe in the Venezuelan jungle. He had married a Huichol Indian and traveled from Canada (his place of origin) to South America, trading Indian handicrafts among the different tribes. He has been doing the yopo snuff ceremonies for some time now.

The ceremony in Belize goes for the symbolic price of 200USD. It includes a tub bath of entheogenic plants in the middle of the night followed by a double ayahuasca-yopo ceremony. While in the bath I listened to the jungle monkeys, the hollering monkeys, wild birds and, lucky me, I heard the jaguar while my skin acted as an absorption membrane for all that entheogenic tea while I melted into the night.

The next morning after my bath of sacred plants, the shaman gave me ayahuasca root bark to chew for an hour on an empty stomach before having the yopo snuff ceremony. When my time came to "blow yopo" (that's the expression), the 5-MeO-DMT–rich snuff, I had the strongest entheogenic experience ever.

The intensity is incomparable; I passed the dome and interacted with interdimensional beings reminding me of my mission and my purpose. I was in awe! Again I was just making the hissing sound *"Sssssssssssss."*

After the ceremony we had an organic dinner. At midnight the shaman woke us up and took us in his truck for a one-hour drive to the Lamanai ruins in Belize. We entered the ruins and climbed the Jaguar Temple. On top of the temple the shaman began another yopo ceremony culminating at sunrise. The shaman called the jaguar, the monkeys, and some fascinating birds. With perfect timing, the light of the next

Sacred Bath Brew composed of ayahuasca, yopo, Hawaiian woodrose, mimosa, and other junge power plants

day appeared over the horizon and we all saw one of the most wonderful sights ever.

During the earlier yopo experience I spent most of the time vomiting in colorful fractals and coughing black phlegm out of my lungs; cleaning my body and my liver. This time it was different since I was already "clean," so my entheogenic experience went beyond my known boundaries. Many times entheogens use emotions to spread their message. Something strong was about to be shown to me. I encountered and interacted with multidimensional Beings of Light. At the time I thought it was a bit aggressive on their part to show me some feelings I did not long for.

I stayed there a couple of days sharing our medicines; the shaman summoned me to his cabin, where we had a very interesting chat. He wanted to have some of my medicine; in exchange he gave me a *costal*, a woven bag of around five kilos of yopo seeds for me to study.

Dr. Gerry and Shaman Chicho Novelo at the Hummingbird Ranch in Belize

I asked him why of all entheogens available he preferred the yopo snuff. He proudly replied: "Dr. Gerry, yopo is guaranteed. Your medicine has the risk of failing if the person coughs or doesn't inhale enough medicine to reach its full effect. Only one intranasal line of my yopo guarantees the entheogenic experience." He smiled and we had a tasty organic joint with a bit of my medicine.

As I returned to Mahahual, I started extracting DMT from various plant sources, not knowing one of the worst hurricanes ever was about to strike our beach.

Hurricane Dean struck the Mahahual coastline on August 22, 2007, destroying the whole town like an atomic bomb. Everything was lost. The navy and army evacuated the town and I had to bail to Palenque for a couple of days of thunderstorms in the Mayan jungle. I returned three days later to find the whole town gone. It felt like Nagasaki or Hiroshima or Chernobyl; simply disaster everywhere. I was so sad to see many ancient trees literally upside down. I lost everything: my house, my office, and my job. The whole town took more than two years to recover from the damage.

I was obliged to look for a job as a general practitioner in Playa del Carmen, Cozumel, and Cancun with no luck. So I applied for a medical specialty and was accepted into the obstetrics and gynecology medical residency at the Women's Hospital in Juarez, Chihuahua, where I lived for six years.

After I finished my medical specialty in obstetrics and gynecology, and my marriage ended abruptly, I returned to my beloved Caribbean.

Living in the magical town of Bacalar, continuing my mission, close to Nature, close to one of the most beautiful water supplies of this planet, spreading the Light, spreading these words, I am fulfilling my destiny. I wish that we continue to spread this Light among us to endure the adversities and heal our planet.

MY STATEMENT

I would like to emphasize the importance of making a statement regarding 5-MeO-DMT.

Once the soul realizes the Ultimate Truth, there can be no lies.

Once one recognizes God in everything, in all the multiverses, then one can only trust and let go. When one has just smoked the golden nectar of a Sonoran Batracius, there is no control; everything is flowing in a direction toward the ultimate understanding of life.

After living these experiences, these feelings, one can only trust the flow and deduce that every single thing that has happened in life has a deep underlying purpose (destiny?).

Ever since my first truly intense entheogenic experience I have come to the realization that I was born for this. It feels very familiar. And that's why I will continue to spread the word and the importance of the entheogenic experience, its potential, its purpose, and its Light. I am willing to take every single action in order to ignite this spark in individuals who eventually will spread this Light as well, to testify in favor of entheogens and mankind's need for them nowadays.

I have mentioned the healing properties of the entheogenic experience; I am not talking about religion, no specific religion whatsoever. It is a path toward the Light of Eternal Love that shines in a unique way.

In conjunction with James Oroc, Martin W. Ball, and Dr. Rettig's opinion that 5-MeO-DMT is the strongest of all entheogens, I firmly trust now is the time and here (this circumstance in human history) is the place to have this kind of experience.

It has the potential to evoke a strong religious cosmic experience in the eyes of the beholder who wishes to enter the void. There can be no ego, no subject, for everything is pure consciousness.

Humanity is in need of a spiritual experience to undo and balance all the cataclysmic planetary mistakes. We have done so much harm to the planet, our home.

It is up to us to stop the material machinery that is killing our Mother Nature, our planet.

The time has come to restore the planetary balance through gaining consciousness by interacting with entheogens that Huxley, Hofmann, Shulgin, Schultes, Leary, and McKenna so widely acclaimed.

The importance of having an entheogenic experience lies in the fact that it is capable of showing us who we really are and what we are made of. As a result, it's most unlikely and improbable that the individual will fall into Babylon's claws again.

After opening one's blinded eyes one can connect with the Source and fulfill his or her own destiny and primal purpose. It goes beyond the material realm, or even the biological system whose only purpose is to perpetuate and evolve our species.

The entheogenic experience is a necessary evolutionary step to surpass the present system's imposed reality, which differs so greatly from our divine purpose. This might just be the molecule capable of changing the world in which we live.

Life is but a blink between two eternities, and if 5-MeO-DMT is capable of elucidating the eternal flame of divine nature that we all possess, then we should definitely find ways to get this medicine to as many people as possible.

Nature is using us to fulfill its purpose. There is nothing artificial; everything is natural and naturally Life will always find a way to manifest its beauty, its magic, the eternal cosmic event that we are all part of.

Dr. Gerry at the Bufo Ranch, 2015

After many years of toad milking in the Sonoran Desert I have observed a drastic drop in the *Bufo alvarius* population. I began by going to localities where these toads reside, and to my surprise I found that not only are they being run over by cars and killed by children, but global warming and a lack of rainfall during the monsoon season are among the main causes of this reduction of specimens.

For the past five years, many young people have been taking these toads out of their natural habitat, which is having a large negative impact on the bufo population as well.

All these findings have led me to create a foundation or civil association to help this species thrive, protect its habitat, raise consciousness among people, and help it reproduce and fulfill its natural place in the circle of Life.

We have successfully created the Bufo Alvarius Foundation in the United States, in Arizona (the American portion of the Sonoran Desert), and La Fundacion Bufo Alvarius AC on the Mexican side, to obtain two large areas where we will help this species complete its life cycle and procure medicine for future generations. It will prevent people from removing the toads and build an ecological space where visitors can learn about and meet these fascinating creatures in their natural habitat.

Our purpose is to work together on both sides of the border running through the Sonoran Desert. We will set up ecological patrols to prevent poachers from harming this wonderful toad, work with local authorities, and raise the general consciousness toward the preservation of the Sonoran Desert toad.

This is just the beginning of a dream. I believe together if we join hands and help we can make it a reality.

TOAD MESSAGE TO THE WORLD

(adapted from a blend of words by
Dr. Rettig and Dr. Sandoval)

God is everywhere in all of us.

We are not only what we eat but also what we see, think, and breathe.

Everything that we introduce to our bodies becomes a part of our physical being.

All the states of consciousness, whether primal, primitive, actual, or futuristic, are linked to language, acquired by entheogens long ago, to achieve the necessary understanding on individual as well as planetary evolution.

Our will, our attitude, and our choice (our energy) are what ultimately transform, impact, affect, and thus create reality all the time beginning with our thoughts and then our breathing.

This medicine is the Light for all people willing to consciously awaken into life. What matters most is the manifestation of the Light and knowledge into our own lives.

This medicine was made for this time, as the Mayans made a prophecy about this time connecting with the Source of Light, the center of the universe. Time kept going on its natural course and made everyone forget this knowledge. The knowledge was encoded by our ancestors into a message that needed to be decoded in a specific point in time: NOW/HERE/TODAY.

We saw the visions to make them into actions in our lives.

This is the message of the toad, an awakening into our own divinity. It is also the message of the planet, our mother. A direct living experience capable of transmitting itself to the Universal Grid of Consciousness where we can hear our ancestors.

Man has discovered cycles. They are all over Nature. Rain cycles control and affect crops and harvests, resulting in fecundity. Men created rituals that celebrated biological and cosmological cycles. Before there were cities, we were nomads and shared ancient knowledge that explained the formation of the world in which we live today. Prior to the formation of books, e-mails, and other means of knowledge transmission, cultures passed on the knowledge through tales and songs.

These were the seeds planted long ago by our ancestors. We are just now collecting the fruits born of these seeds, which is why the toad medicine is appearing now, and not before. Everything comes out right on time, neither before nor after. Everything is perfect. Now is the time for this magical sacred medicine.

We see Light everywhere. We are Light. Let's shine on, brothers and sisters!

BIBLIOGRAPHY

Davis, W., and A. Weil. "Identity of a New World Psycho-active Toad." *Ancient Mesoamerica* 3 (1) (1992), 51–59.

Eliade, M. *Shamanism: Archaic Techniques of Ecstasy.* London: Routledge & Kegan Paul. 1964.

Erspamer, V., et al. "5-Methoxy-and 5-hydroxiindoles in the skin of *Bufo alvarius*." *Biochemical Pharmacology* 16 (7) (1967), 1149–64.

Franzen, Fr., and H. Gross. "Tryptamine, N, N-Dimethyl-tryptamine, N, N,-Dimethyl 5- hydroxytryptamine and 5-Methoxytryptamine in Human Blood and Urine." *Nature* 206 (1965), 1052.

Grey, A. *Sacred Mirrors: The Visionary Art of Alex Grey.* Rochester, Vt.: Inner Traditions, 1990.

Haisch, B. *The God Theory: Universes, Zero-Point Fields, and What's Behind It All.* York Beach, Me.: Red Wheel/Weiser, 2006.

Hamblin, N. L. "The Magic Toads of Cozumel." *Mexicon* 3 (1) (1979), 10–14.

Hartmann, T. *The Last Hours of Ancient Sunlight: The Fate of the World and What We Can Do Before It's Too Late*. New York: Three Rivers Press, 1998.

Horowitz, M. and C. Palmer. *Moksha: Aldous Huxley's Classic Writing on Psychedelics and the Visionary Experience*. Rochester, Vt.: Park Street Press, 1977/1999.

Hoshino, T., and K. Shimodaira. "Uber die Synthesedes Bufotenin-Methyl-Athers (5 Methoxy-N,Dimethyl-Tryptamin) und Bufotenins (Synthesen in der Indol-Gruppe. XV)." *Bulletin of the Chemical Society of Japan* 11 (3) (1936), 221–24.

Huxley, A. *The Doors of Perception*. New York: Harper & Brothers Publishers, 1954.

———. *Heaven and Hell*. New York: Harper & Brothers Publishers, 1955.

Laszlo E. *Third Millennium: The Challenge and the Vision*. London: Gaia Books Limited, 1997.

———. *The Connectivity Hypothesis: Foundations of an Integral Science of Quantum, Cosmos, Life, and Consciousness*. Albany, N.Y.: State University of New York Press, 2003.

———. *Science and the Akashic Field: An Integral Theory of Everything.* Rochester, Vt.: Inner Traditions, 2004.

Levi, E. *The Great Secret: Or Occultism Unveiled.* Kier Edit. Buenos Aires, 1995.

Lopez Amaro, Gerardo. *Diario de Campo Historia de El paraje del Coyote, San Antonio de Coronados.* San Luis Potosi, 2008.

Lyttle, T., et al. "Bufo Toads and Bufotenine: Fact and Fiction Surrounding an Alleged Psychedelic." *Journal of Psychoactive Drugs* 28 (3) (1996), 267–90.

Manske, R. H. F. "A Synthesis of the Methyltryptamines and Some Derivatives." *Canadian Journal of Research* 5 (1931), 592–600.

McTaggart, L. *The Field: The Quest for the Secret Force of the Universe.* New York: Harper Perennial, 2003.

Most, A. *Bufo Alvarius: The Psychedelic Toad of the Sonoran Desert.* Denton, Tex.: Venom Press, 1984.

Ogarrio Perkins, C. E. *Cantos de los COMCAAC, El legado de los Barnett.* Hermosillo, Sonora: Jorale Editores, 2011.

Oroc, J. *Tryptamine Palace: 5 MeO-DMT and the Bufo Alvarius Toad: A Journey from Burning Man to the Akashic Field.* Rochester, Vt.: Park Street Press, 2009.

Popp, F-A. "Coupling of Fröhlich-Modes as a Basis of Biological Regulation." In *Herbert Fröhlich, FRS: A Physicist Ahead of His Time: A Centennial Celebration of His Life and Work*. G. J. Hyland and P. Rowlands, eds. Liverpool, England: The University of Liverpool, 2005.

Robicsek, Francis and Donald M. Hales. *The Maya Book of the Dead: The Ceramic Codex*. Charlottesville: University Museum of Virginia, 1981.

Schultes, R. E., and A. Hofmann. *The Botany and Chemistry of Hallucinogens*, Second Edition, Springfield, Ill.: Charles C. Thomas, 1980.

Shulgin, Alexander, and Ann Shulgin. *PIHKAL: A Chemical Love Story*. Berkeley, Calif.: Transform Press, 1991.

———. *TIHKAL: The Continuation*. Berkeley, Calif.: Transform Press, 1997.

Sogyal, R. *The Tibetan Book of Living and Dying, Revised and Updated*. San Francisco: Harper San Francisco, 2002.

Strassman, R. *DMT: The Spirit Molecule: A Doctor's Revolutionary Research into the Biology of Near-Death Experiences*. Rochester, Vt.: Park Street Press, 2001.

Wasson. R. G., et al. "The Road to Eleusis: Unveiling the Secret of the Mysteries." *Ethnomycological Studies No. 4*. New York: Harcourt Brace Jovanovich, 1978.

Zohar, D. *The Quantum Self: Human Nature and Consciousness Defined by the New Physics*. New York: Quill/William Morrow, 1990.

VAPORIZING 5-MeO-DMT FROM *BUFO ALVARIUS* AS AN ENTHEOGEN:

A RETROSPECTIVE CASE CONTROL STUDY

Gerardo Ruben Sandoval Isaac, MD, OB-GYN

※

SUMMARY

The objective of this study is to present the results of a 10-year period of administering the secretion of the *Bufo alvarius* toad's gland by means of vaporization, to induce an entheogenic experience.

Sixteen hundred individuals were exposed to a dose ranging from 20–250mg of vaporized dried toad venom. A short medical interview was given to all participants to assess risk and decide whether or not they were suitable for such experience. Of noted importance was religion, actual belief system, history of surgical procedures, known illnesses, intake of medications, history of drug use, experience in psychedelics, and underlying medical conditions.

The ages ranged from 17–96 years old. The mean duration of the experience was 20 +- 10 minutes with a minimum time frame of 5 minutes and a maximum of 57 minutes.

All subjects were not exposed to a MAO inhibitor 2 weeks prior to the intake of the toad venom. They were advised not to engage in sexual activity 3 days prior, no meat or preserved products intake, and not to take any drugs or mind-altering substances prior to the experience.

Among the medical background, subjects with AIDS, cancer, multiple sclerosis, autoimmune disorders, diabetes, high blood pressure, depression, thyroid disease, drug abuse intake were not excluded from the study. On the other hand, people with mental diseases such as schizoid disorders, schizophrenia, and other psychiatric diseases were excluded. People who took MAO inhibitors 2 weeks prior to the experience were excluded from this study.

MATERIALS AND METHODS

A recompilation of information gathered in personal notes taken from the experiences recorded from 2005 to 2015, the use of medical devices such as a pulse oxymeter, and sphygmomanometer were applied in some cases. The use of a video camera was used only if the participant desired. A hand chronometer was used to measure the time frame of the exposure.

A requirement of holding the vaporized substance inside the lungs for 10 seconds and not having coughed while the intake took place was suggested in order to evaluate the full effect of the substance on the body.

All information was gathered and entered into a database.

The set and setting were of vital importance in the realization of this experience. Special attention was paid to creating a safe site, with an adjustable position, reinforced pillow, warm blankets, an empty bucket if nausea or vomiting presented, and plenty of water.

A small integration period post exposure occurred to analyze the process, by means of sharing both the participant's and facilitator's account of events.

Each participant was given a crystal lollipop pipe or oil burner as the device to administer the toad venom. A torch lighter was used to vaporize the material and as soon as the vapors filled the device, the participant was asked to take a single inhalation lasting from 5 to 8 seconds. The pipe was removed carefully and the participant was asked to lie down, palms upward, legs lightly bent and spread.

Immediately, the 10-second countdown began and the chronometer was set.

After, the participant was allowed to release the fumes.

The participant was asked to advise when reincorporation took place in order to start the integration process (this term is applied when the participant feels that he/she is back to his/her body and in this reality).

The integration process consists of asking if the participant remembers the process, the presence of colors or visions, or sensations that arise during the process. An analysis was made of what body movements manifested, if they were unilateral or bilateral, and if there was any contraction or muscle spasm. Personal recommendations were shared regarding the experience and all participants were told to keep in contact and share their integration process in the following days or month post exposure, and to ask for any assistance if needed.

RESULTS

A total of 1600 participants who met the inclusion criteria were enrolled in this study. All of them were exposed to a dose ranging from 20–250mg of vaporized dried toad venom.

The age ranged from 17–96 years old. The mean duration of the experience was 20 +- 10 minutes with a minimum time frame of 5 minutes and a maximum of 57 minutes.

No subjects were exposed to an MAO inhibitor 2 weeks prior to the intake of the toad venom.

70% were males, 30% were females.

5 persons out of 1600 did not experience any effect upon exposure and curiously they were all Austrians.

25% of females experienced a tantric sexual orgasm experience.

85% of the participants experienced a mystical/religious experience.

60% experienced some form of dying or death.

15% presented nausea or vomiting.

7% presented problems in sleeping, or anxiety post exposure resolving within a month and responding favorably to integrating methods such as: grounding foods, acupuncture, hot and cold baths, yoga and breath work, rigorous physical exercise, touch and being held, herbal sleep remedies, and less frequent sedatives or psychotherapy.

30% presented similar outbursts of flashbacks with severe intensity.

An insignificant elevation of the blood pressure and heartbeat was noted prior to the experience and during the first 3 minutes.

There was a decreased oxygen saturation levels during the peak experience but it never reached <88% in participants whose oxygen saturation was measured using a laser pulsometer.

The dose required to reach threshold experience was 100mg. The dose that manifested retroactive amnesia was >120mg. The dose required for mild to moderate psychedelic effects ranged from 50 to 70mg. The minimum experience dose was 20mg.

A direct proportional relationship between history of psychedelics and time frame of the experience was noted, the more experienced the less time.

There is a significant positive effect regarding the exposure of this substance. There was a positive quality of life reported in the first month post exposure.

There is a significant mental stability obtained by a single exposure to this substance reported as increased stamina and heightened mind ability to resolve problems.

There is a significant report of entheogenic experiences reached through the vaporization of the bufo toad's secretion.

There is a significant increase in improving social interaction and better understanding of the self, induced by this experience.

A significant number of participants reported it as the strongest religious experience of their lives; a significant number even claimed to have reached enlightenment.

A significant number of people reported this to be the peak experience of their lives.

OBSERVATIONS

The personality of the participant and their nature and past-lived events condition the experience.

Having a background of spirituality leads to more positive outcomes.

There seems to be a better understanding of the abstract terms and the nature of Life after a single exposure to this compound.

The mind is very powerful in the way that it can interfere and limit the absorption of this compound.

Difficulties in the integration period are more common in people with strong materialistic personalities, people who are living a life that they did not want for themselves, people who are unhappy with their current state or situation, or people who have been living for years a reality that differs to their true nature or dreams.

The total dissolution of the ego is needed for a true entheogenic effect and to reach the full potential or effect of this substance. Different people experience different levels of entheogenic effect due to their own personal, intellectual, and spiritual development.

Not everyone will have a full mystical experience from smoking toad medicine.

SERI CHANTS

FROM THE COMCA'AC NATION, PUNTA CHUECA, SONORA, MEXICO

by Chief Elder Francisco Barnett Astorga

Hant i tcoo iya
Hant i tcoo iya
Tamepit Temoya

Ketso jamepe te hanzo heya
Ketso Jaxema mane Tanzo heya
Te kompenza heya
Tebe Tebe Tenaimo
Hant icaheme toii yopot i
Hant icaheme toii yopot i
Hant com tcooo toii yopot i
Hamiime imac toii yopot i
Hant com timoz iya toii yopot i

Eke kesto jaxema heya
Eke sakame heya

Me kanzo heya
Te kompenza heya
Kesto jaxema heya ya
Kesto jamepe ya
Te mamepe temoya
Te kompenza heya
Te kompenza heya
Mamepe temoya
Oka Toyopotei
Ajatipe

Yooz quihj mizj masaai: "God bless you"
Yooz quihj mizj mazi saatim: "God bless you (plural)"
Ajatipe: "thank you"
Laak: "brother"

DR. GERRY'S INVOCATION

This is the prayer that I say before I begin my ceremonies. It has helped and protected throughout my journey.

Mother, Father God/Goddess,
great infinite spirit, angels,

Light workers, spirit guides,
transdimensional beings of light,

Knowing we are all one, and knowing
that all we need to do is ask

and we shall receive:

So at this time I am asking for your
presence, divine spirit

To fill this space, filling my mind,
my body, and my soul

Allowing me to be a clear, open channel of
your infinite light, love, wisdom, healing
energies, and the Christ consciousness.

As I feel your presence, I give thanks.

Welcome! Welcome to all those of the higher realms!

I thank you for your loving, compassionate,
and joyful participation.

Today I thank you, Mother Earth, Father Sun-
god, for the healing of myself and others
and the healing of Mother Earth.

Peace on Earth begins today, and it begins within me.

I accept that I am a divine child of God.

It is safe for me to feel all my feelings.

I will **release, relax, and allow**
divine love to enter me.

Ahoo

ABOUT THE AUTHOR

Doctor, gynecologist, and "medicine man" GERARDO RUBEN SANDOVAL ISAAC, MD, OB-GYN was born in Guadalajara, Mexico. He has lived in and frequently visits his properties at Real de Catorce and San Jose Pacifico, in Mexico. He has lived in Nepal, India, Germany, Palenque, Cozumel, Mahahual, Playa del Carmen, Juarez, Chetumal, and Bacalar. He has been sharing the entheogenic experience as an MD in Magical Mexico since 2005, and performs entheogenic ceremonies around the world. He actively fights to spread the legal medical and ritual use of cannabis and all entheogens in Mexico. He is the founding member and director of the Bufo Alvarius Foundation Corp. in the US, and founding member and president of Fundacion Bufo Alvarius in Mexico;

both nonprofit organizations focus on protecting the Sonoran Desert toad on both sides of the border of the Sonoran Desert.

Dr. Gerardo Sandoval lives in the Sonoran Desert, where he is trying to build a research facility and a toad sanctuary to protect the Sonoran Desert toad.

The author can be contacted at
bufoalvariustoads@gmail.com

Transforming self. Celebrating life.

Divine Arts was created five years ago to share some of the new and ancient knowledge that is rapidly emerging from the indigenous and wisdom cultures of the world; and to present new voices that express eternal truths in innovative and accessible ways.

We have realized from the shifts in our own consciousness that millions of people worldwide are simultaneously expanding their awareness and experiencing the multi-dimensional nature of reality.

Our authors, masters and teachers from around the world, have come together from all spiritual practices to create Divine Arts books. Our unity comes in celebrating the sacredness of life, and having the intention that our work will assist in raising our consciousness which will ultimately benefit all sentient beings.

We trust that these books will serve you on whatever path you journey, and we welcome hearing from you.

Michael Wiese and Geraldine Overton,
Publishers

mw@mwp.com   *glow@blue-earth.co.uk*

Printed in the USA
CPSIA information can be obtained
at www.ICGtesting.com
JSHW082338140824
68134JS00020B/1746